Scrum - A Pocket Guide
2nd edition

D0876260

Other publications by Van Haren Publishing

Van Haren Publishing (VHP) specializes in titles on Best Practices, methods and standards within four domains:
- IT and IT Management
- Architecture (Enterprise and IT)
- Business Management and
- Project Management

Van Haren Publishing is also publishing on behalf of leading organizations and companies: ASLBiSL Foundation, BRMI, CA, Centre Henri Tudor, Gaming Works, IACCM, IAOP, IFDC, Innovation Value Institute, IPMA-NL, ITSqc, NAF, KNVI, PMI-NL, PON, The Open Group, The SOX Institute.

Topics are (per domain):

IT and IT Management	Enterprise Architecture	Project Management
ABC of ICT	ArchiMate®	A4-Projectmanagement
ASL®	GEA®	DSDM/Atern
CATS CM®	Novius Architectuur	ICB / NCB
CMMI®	Methode	ISO 21500
COBIT®	TOGAF®	MINCE®
e-CF		M_o_R®
ISO/IEC 20000	**Business Management**	MSP®
ISO/IEC 27001/27002	BABOK® Guide	P3O®
ISPL	BiSL® and BiSL® Next	PMBOK® Guide
IT4IT®	BRMBOK™	Praxis®
IT-CMF™	BTF	PRINCE2®
IT Service CMM	EFQM	
ITIL®	eSCM	
MOF	IACCM	
MSF	ISA-95	
SABSA	ISO 9000/9001	
SAF	OPBOK	
SIAM™	SixSigma	
TRIM	SOX	
VeriSM™	SqEME®	

For the latest information on VHP publications, visit our website: www.vanharen.net.

Scrum

A Pocket Guide
2nd edition

A Smart Travel Companion

Van Haren
PUBLISHING

Colophon

Title:	Scrum - A Pocket Guide - 2nd edition
Subtitle:	A Smart Travel Companion
Author:	Gunther Verheyen
Reviewers:	Ken Schwaber (Scrum co-creator, Scrum.org)
	David Starr (Agile Craftsman, Microsoft)
	Ralph Jocham (Agile Professional, effective agile.)
	Patricia M. Kong (Business Agility Enterprise Solutions, Scrum.org)
	Blake McMillan (Scrum Master – soulofscrum.com)
	Dominik Maximini (Agile Lead, NovaTec Consulting GmbH)
Publisher:	Van Haren Publishing, 's Hertogenbosch, www.vanharen.net
ISBN hard copy:	978 94 018 0375 5
ISBN eBook (pdf):	978 94 018 0376 2
ISBN ePUB:	978 94 018 0377 9
Edition:	Second edition, first impression, January 2019
Layout and typesetting:	Coco Bookmedia, Amersfoort - NL
Copyright:	Gunther Verheyen & Van Haren Publishing

Foreword by Ken Schwaber

An outstanding accomplishment that simmers with intelligence.

Scrum – A Pocket Guide is an extraordinarily competent book. Gunther has described everything about Scrum in well-formed, clearly written descriptions that flow with insight, understanding, and perception. Yet, you are never struck by these attributes. You simply benefit from them, later thinking, "That was really, really helpful. I found what I needed to know, readily understood what I wanted, and wasn't bothered by irrelevancies."

I have struggled to write this foreword. I feel the foreword should be as well-written as the book it describes. In this case, that is hard. Read Gunther's book. Read it in part, or read it in whole. You will be satisfied.

Scrum is simple, but complete and competent in addressing complex problems. Gunther's pocket guide is complete and competent in addressing understanding a simple framework for addressing complex problems, Scrum.

Ken, 22 August 2013

Preface

The use of Agile methods continues to gain traction with Scrum as the most widely adopted definition of Agile. The general level of interest in Scrum is already huge, yet still growing, in and beyond software development.

Transforming an organization's way of working to Scrum represents quite a challenge. Scrum is not a cookbook 'process' with detailed and exhaustive prescriptions for every imaginable situation. Scrum is a *framework* of principles, rules and values that thrives on the *people* employing Scrum. A major potential of Scrum lies in the discovery and *emergence* of practices, tools and techniques and in optimizing them for each specific context.

The benefits realized through Scrum depend on the will to remove barriers, think across walls and separations, and embark on a journey of discovery. Scrum is more about behavior than it is about process.

The journey starts by understanding the rules of Scrum to start playing Scrum. This book aspires to be your companion along the way, all the way. This book shows how Scrum implements the Agile mindset, what the rules of the game of Scrum are, and how these rules leave room for a variety of tactics to play the game. The ambition of introducing all these aspects is to make this book a worthwhile read for people, teams, managers and change agents, whether they are already doing Scrum or want to embark on their journey of Scrum.

In 2003 my journey took off. My path of agility started with eXtreme Programming and Scrum. It has inevitably been a cobblestone path. On my journey I have used Scrum with many teams, in various projects and initiatives, at different scales and at different organizations. I have worked with both large and small enterprises and have coached individual practitioners and teams as well as executive management. I created the first edition of this book, '*Scrum - A Pocket Guide*'. I was in the fortunate position of partnering with Ken Schwaber, co-creator of Scrum, at Scrum.org, while also shepherding their 'Professional' series of Scrum trainings, courseware and assessments. I am gratified to continue my journey of Scrum as an independent Scrum Caretaker.

Who would have figured that there was demand for a second edition of my pocket guide to Scrum, five years after the almost accidental creation of the first edition in 2013?

I consider how I described the Scrum Values in the first edition. In July 2016 they were added to the Scrum Guide. I described the traditional 3 questions as a good, but optional tactic to use at the Daily Scrum. That too was added to the Scrum Guide, in November 2017.

However, more and bigger challenges have surfaced since 2013. The balance of society keeps drastically and rapidly shifting from industrial (often physical) labor to digital (often virtual) work. In many domains of society, the unpredictability of work increases continually. The industrial paradigm is rendered useless, definitely. The need for the Agile paradigm is bigger than ever, and thus the need for the tangible framework of Scrum to help people and organizations increase their agility in performing complex work in complex circumstances.

Scrum is increasingly being discovered as *a simple framework to address complex challenges*, more than as a way to deliver complex (software) products. More and different people ask for guidance and insights on their journey of Scrum in domains beyond software development. It required a more generic description of the rules of Scrum, different words, other angles to the same set of rules. Organizations look for clear insights in the simple rules of Scrum as they envision re-emerging their structures and their way of working around Scrum. As the third Scrum wave is rising, this second edition introduces or refreshes the simplicity of Scrum for those that want to surf that wave. This second edition offers the foundational insights into Scrum for them and their organizations to properly shape their Scrum.

I thank Ken for the foreword and his review for the original (2013) edition as well as the other reviewers Dave Starr, Patricia Kong and Ralph Jocham for their feedback on that first edition. I thank Blake McMillan and Dominik Maximini for their much-appreciated review of this second edition. I thank all translators for their past and on-going efforts to spread my words in different languages. I thank all at Van Haren Publishing, and especially Ivo van Haren, for giving me the chance to express my views on Scrum with this book.

Enjoy reading, and... keep Scrumming.

Gunther, June 2013 / August 2018

Reviews

This Scrum Pocket Guide is outstanding. It is well organized, well written, and the content is excellent. This should be the de facto standard handout for all looking for a complete, yet clear overview of Scrum.

(Ken Schwaber, Scrum co-creator, August 2013)

Gunther has expertly packaged the right no-nonsense guidance for teams seeking agility, without a drop of hyperbole. This is the book about agility with Scrum I wish I had written.

(David Starr, Agile Craftsman, June 2013)

During my many Scrum training activities I often get asked: "For Scrum, what is the one book to read?" In the past the answer wasn't straightforward, but now it is! The Scrum Pocket Guide is the one book to read when starting with Scrum. It is a concise, yet complete and passionate reference about Scrum.

(Ralph Jocham, Agile Professional, effective agile., June 2013)

"The house of Scrum is a warm house. It's a house where people are WELCOME." Gunther's passion for Scrum and its players is evident in his work and in each chapter of this book. He explains the Agile paradigm, lays

out the Scrum framework and then discusses the 'future state of Scrum.' Intimately, in about 100 pages.

(Patricia M. Kong, Business Agility Enterprise Solutions, Scrum.org, June 2013)

I recommend reading *Scrum – A Pocket Guide* early in your Scrum journey to help you gain a deeper understanding of why Scrum works and how the values and principles can positively impact the lives of your team as well as the health of an organization. Reading it later in your journey is great too… except for the feeling of regret wishing you had read it earlier.

(Blake McMillan, Scrum Master – Soulofscrum.com, August 2018)

It is hard to find concise, to the point literature about Scrum. Most authors circle around the core topics instead of naming them. Gunther chose to break this pattern, enlightening us with the knowledge of the truly important parts of Scrum. When starting on your Scrum journey, make sure to take a copy of this guide along with you.

(Dominik Maximini, Agile Lead, NovaTec Consulting GmbH, August 2018)

Table of contents

1   THE AGILE PARADIGM **15**

    1.1   To shift or not to shift............................... 15

    1.2   The origins of Agile 20

    1.3   Definition of Agile 21

    1.4   The iterative-incremental continuum...................... 24

    1.5   Agility can't be planned............................. 27

    1.6   Combining Agile and Lean............................ 30

2   SCRUM **39**

    2.1   The house of Scrum 39

    2.2   Scrum, what's in a name? 40

    2.3   Is that a gorilla I see over there?...................... 43

    2.4   Framework, not methodology 47

    2.5   Playing the game................................... 49

    2.6   Core principles of Scrum............................. 63

    2.7   The Scrum values 73

3   TACTICS FOR A PURPOSE **79**

    3.1   Visualizing progress................................. 80

    3.2   The Daily Scrum questions............................ 82

    3.3   Product Backlog refinement 83

    3.4   User Stories 84

3.5   Planning Poker 85
3.6   Sprint length 86
3.7   How Scrum scales. 88

4   THE FUTURE STATE OF SCRUM 95
4.1   Yes, we do Scrum. And... 95
4.2   The power of the possible product 97
4.3   The upstream adoption of Scrum 99

ANNEXES 105
Annex A: Scrum Glossary 105
Annex B: References 109
About the author 113

1 The Agile paradigm

■ 1.1 TO SHIFT OR NOT TO SHIFT

The software industry was for a long time dominated by a paradigm of *industrial* views and beliefs. This was in fact a copy-paste of old manufacturing routines and theories. An essential element in this landscape of knowledge, views and practices was the Taylorist[1] conviction that 'workers' can't be trusted to intelligently, autonomously and creatively perform their work. They are expected to only carry out pre-defined, executable tasks. Their work must be prepared, designed and planned by more senior staff. And then still, hierarchical supervisors must vigilantly oversee the execution of these carefully prepared tasks. Quality is assured

Figure 1.1 The industrial paradigm

by admitting the good and rejecting the bad batches of outputs. Monetary rewards are used to stimulate desired behavior. Unwanted behavior is punished. The old 'carrots and sticks' strategies.

The serious flaws of the old paradigm in software development are known and well documented. In particular, the Chaos reports of the Standish Group [Standish, 2011; Standish, 2013] have over and over revealed the low success rates of traditional software development. Many shortcomings and errors resulting from the application of the industrial paradigm in software development are well beyond reasonable levels of tolerance. The unfortunate response seems to have been to lower expectations. It became accepted that only 10-20% of software projects were successful. The definition of 'success' in the industrial paradigm is made up of the combination of on-time, within budget and including all scope. *Although these criteria for success can be disputed, it is the paradigm's promise.* It became accepted that quality is low, and that over 50% of features of traditionally delivered software applications are never used [Standish, 2002; Standish, 2013].

Although it is not widely and consciously admitted, the industrial paradigm did put the software industry in a serious crisis. Many tried to overcome this crisis by fortifying the industrial approach. More plans were created, more phases scheduled, more designs made, more work was done upfront, hoping that the actual work would be executed more effectively. The exhaustiveness of the upfront work was increased. The core idea remained that the 'workers' needed to be directed, but with even more detailed instructions. Supervision was increased and intensified. *As the success rates did not increase, the industrial paradigm assumes that the instructions are not clear and detailed enough.*

Yet, little improved. Many flaws, defects and low quality remained and had to be tolerated.

It took some time, but inevitably new ideas and insights started forming upon observing the significant anomalies of the industrial paradigm.

The seeds of a new world view were already sown in the 1990's. But it was in 2001 that these resulted in the formal naming of 'Agile', a turning-point in the history of software development. A new paradigm was born, in the realm of the software industry but in the meantime expanding to other domains of society. It is a paradigm that thrives upon heuristics and creativity, a paradigm that thrives upon the (restored) respect for the creative nature of the work and the intelligence of the 'workers'.

Figure 1.2 The Agile paradigm

The software industry has good reasons to keep moving to the new paradigm; the existing flaws are significant, widely known and the presence of software in society grows exponentially, making it a critical aspect of our modern world. However, by definition, a shift to a new paradigm takes time. And the old paradigm seems to have deep roots and a considerable half-life time. An industrial approach to software development continues to be taught and promoted as the most appropriate one.

Many say that Agile is too radical and they, therefore, propagate a gradual introduction of Agile practices within the existing, traditional frames. However, there is reason to be very skeptical about such gradual evolution, a slow progression from the old to the new paradigm, from waterfall to Agile.

The chances are high that a gradual evolution will never go beyond the surface, will not do more than just scratch that surface. New names will be installed, new terms and new practices will be imposed, but the fundamental thinking and behavior of people and organizations remain the same. Essential flaws remain untouched; especially the disrespect for people that leads to the continued treatment of creative, intelligent people as mindless 'workers', as 'resources'.

The preservation of the traditional foundations will keep existing data, metrics and standards in place, and the new paradigm will be measured against those old standards. Different paradigms by their nature however consist of fundamentally different concepts and ideas, generally mutually exclusive. No meaningful comparison between the industrial and the Agile paradigm is possible. It requires the honesty to accept the serious flaws of the old ways. It requires leadership, vision, entrepreneurship and persistence to embrace the new ways, thereby abandoning the old thinking.

A gradual shift is factually a status-quo situation that keeps the industrial paradigm intact.

There is overwhelming evidence that the old paradigm doesn't work. Much of the evidence on Agile used to be anecdotal, personal or relatively minor. The Chaos report of 2011 by the Standish Group [Standish, 2011] marked a turning point, holding clear research results for the first time that were confirmed in all later Chaos reports. Extensive research was done in comparing traditional projects with projects that used Agile methods. The report shows that an Agile approach results in a much higher yield, even against the old expectations that software must be delivered on time, on budget and with all the promised scope. The report shows that the Agile projects were three times as successful, and there were three times fewer failed Agile projects compared to traditional projects. For large projects however, the changes in success rates were less outspoken, which is likely more about starting with the wrong expectations in the large, i.e. the combination of time+budget+scope. Against the right expectations, with a focus on active customer collaboration and frequent delivery of value, the new paradigm would be performing even better, with vertical slices of value, frequently delivered, to overcome the volume problem.

Yet, Agile is a choice, not a must. It is one way to improve the software industry. Research shows it is more successful.

 Scrum helps.

The distinct rules of Scrum help in getting a grip on the new paradigm. The small set of prescriptions allows immediate action and results in a more fruitful absorption of the new paradigm. Scrum is a tangible way to adopt the Agile paradigm. Using Scrum, people do develop new ways of working; through discovery, experimentation-based learning and collaboration. They enter a new state of being, a state of *agility*; a state of constant change, flux, evolution and adaptation. This process helps their organizations transform towards such a *state* of agility, freeing up time, people and energy for being innovative (again).

Nevertheless, despite its practicality, experience shows that adopting Scrum often represents a giant leap. This may be because of the uncertainty induced by letting go of old certainties, even if those old certainties have proven not to be very reliable. It may be the time that it takes to make a substantial shift. It may be the determination and hard work that is required. Over and over again it is shown that Scrum is simple, not easy.

■ 1.2   THE ORIGINS OF AGILE

Despite the domination of the plan-driven, industrial views, an evolutionary approach to software development is not new. Craig Larman has extensively described the historical predecessors of Agile in his book *'Agile & Iterative Development, A Manager's Guide'* [Larman, 2004].

But the official label 'Agile' dates from February 2001, when 17 software development leaders gathered at the Snowbird ski resort in Utah. They discussed their views on software development in times when the failing waterfall approaches were replaced by heavy-weight RUP implementations ('Rational Unified Process'), which did not lead to better results than the traditional processes. These development leaders were following different paths and methods, each being a distinct implementation of the new paradigm; Scrum, eXtreme Programming, Adaptive Software Development, Crystal, Feature Driven Development, etc.

The gathering resulted in assigning the label 'Agile' to the common principles, beliefs and thinking of these leaders and their methods. They were published as the *'Manifesto for Agile Software Development'* [Beck, et.al., 2001].

Often the desire "to do Agile" can be overheard. And all too often it is the desire for a magical solution, another silver bullet process that solves all problems. It makes me often state that *"Agile does not exist"*. Agile is not one fixed process, method or practice. Agile is the collection of principles that the methods for Agile software development have in common. Agile refers to the mindset, the convictions and the preferences expressed in the Manifesto for Agile Software Development.

The manifesto does help to grasp the ideas underpinning Agile. If you use it as a source to gain a deeper understanding of Agile, then I strongly advise looking at the 12 principles behind the 4 value statements, see http://agilemanifesto.org/principles.html.

We are uncovering better ways of developing
software by doing it and helping others do it.
Through this work we have come to value:

Individuals and interactions over processes and tools
Working software over comprehensive documentation
Customer collaboration over contract negotiation
Responding to change over following a plan

That is, while there is value in the items on
the right, we value the items on the left more.

Figure 1.3 The Agile Manifesto

■ 1.3 DEFINITION OF AGILE

In the absence of a concise specific definition I prefer describing 'Agile' in
terms of three key characteristics. These are the traits that are common to
the portfolio of Agile methods and are typical to an Agile way of working:

- People driven;
- Iterative-incremental process;
- Value, the measure of success.

1.3.1 People driven

Agile is not driven by a predictive plan on how to implement requirements
that were exhaustively analyzed, designed and architected in an upfront
way. Agile acknowledges that requirements cannot be predicted in every
possible detail in an upfront way.

Agile is not a process of handing over different types of intermediate
deliverables to different specialist departments, where each department
performs its specialized work in isolation.

Agile is driven by the continuous *collaboration* of people ranging over all
required departments; whether they are called business, IT, marketing,
sales, customer service, operations or management. Agile certainly does not

recognize the traditional business versus IT discord. The two are needed for success, from the perspective of creating both useable *and* useful software products, software that is valuable.

Collaboration, interaction and conversation call for a different management style to be effective. Agile teams are *facilitated* through servant-leadership. Boundaries and a context for self-management exist, upon which teams are given objectives and direction. Subtle control emerges from the boundaries.

Collaboration and facilitation replace the traditional command-and-control mechanisms of instructing individuals on a daily basis with executable micro-tasks and totalitarian authorities for invasive control.

This expresses how people are respected for their creativity, intelligence and self-organizing capabilities. People are respected for their ability to understand and resolve a problem without being overloaded with tons of ceremony and bureaucracy. A ceremonial overload only replaces the collaborative thinking, innovation and accountability of people with bureaucracy, paper results, hand-overs and administrative excuses.

People are respected in the time they can spend on their work via the idea of *Sustainable Pace*. Work is organized in such a way that the tempo is sustainable, indefinitely.

1.3.2   Iterative-incremental process
Agile processes are not free-play approaches. Agile processes are *defined* and require high *discipline*.

Products are created piece by piece ('incremental') with each piece being made up of expansions, improvements, eliminations and modifications. The built pieces and the total product are frequently revisited ('iterative') to assure overall integrity.

Agile requires explicit attention from all players on quality and excellence. Agile replaces the idea that these can simply be poured into documents and paper descriptions that have very different properties than the envisioned final result, the releasable product.

The need for an iterative-incremental process is augmented by the finding that requirements and implementation, no matter how much time, energy and funding are spent on predicting them in an upfront way, are prone to change. Markets and competitors evolve, users only know what they want when they get to use it, enterprise strategies change, to name just a few. It calls for an extreme awareness and openness for change.

Contrary to a predictive process, change is not excluded from the Agile process nor expelled to the ceremonial outskirts of development. New insights, evolving opinions and changed priorities form the living heart of Agile. Agile thrives upon emergence, the emergence and subsequent gradual evolution of requirements, plans, ideas, architectures and designs. Change is not disruptive because it forms a natural part of the way of working. Agile *encourages* change as a source of innovation and improvement.

1.3.3   Value, the measure of success

Progress in development cannot be measured and guaranteed on the basis of mere compliance with predictive plans and milestones, documents, hand-overs, signatures, approvals or other ceremonial obligations as is the case in the industrial paradigm. Agile introduces new ways of measuring progress and success.

Agile makes it explicit that progress and success can only be determined by frequently inspecting *working versions of* product (not intermediate descriptions of it) and the actual *value* the product holds for the people who will use it.

It is a natural part of product development that the people having to use the product can only be sure about the usability and usefulness when they actually get their hands on it. No paper documentation or virtual process can replace this. It is an invitation for an iterative-incremental process, for closing the feedback loop with users regularly and measuring the impact and appreciation as an import source of information for further product evolutions.

■ 1.4   THE ITERATIVE-INCREMENTAL CONTINUUM

An Agile approach slices time into time-boxed iterations, periods having a fixed start and end date. There are many advantages to the technique of time-boxing, with *focus* being an important one. This time management technique allows the absorption of pivots or disruptive changes, as well as ensures regular checks so that lessons learned can be incorporated from one iteration to the next in a situation of more continuous flow. The core objective of each iteration is to create versions of valuable, working versions of product no later than at the end of it in order to gather feedback and enable early learning.

In Agile all development work is reorganized to optimize the ability to respond to and capitalize on *business* opportunities.

'Value' is the answer to user, market and business demands and the overall measure of progress and success. Value is an internal assumption within the organization until the product is actually released to the marketplace. Releasing product versions to the marketplace is the only way to validate the assumption of value. Releasing to the marketplace regularly is the only way to adapt to the feedback and appreciation, or lack there-off, of the marketplace. This is done in subsequent evolutions of the product. Value is continuously optimized across iterations. Risk is controlled by consecutively producing working increments based upon defined development standards.

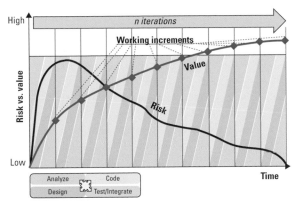

Figure 1.4 Agile Value Delivery

'Risk' also relates to the business perspective. Bear in mind that, certainly in an IT context, risk is typically defined as something technical (*Will the system perform? Is the system scalable?*). It covers the aspect of a product being *usable* (*Will it technically hold? Not break?*). But a mere technical or development perspective on risk often ignores the fact that the ultimate goal of Agile development is to provide greater satisfaction with end-users and customers, to ensure that the products are *useful*. A product being usable from a technical perspective on risk is just the beginning,

Any modern development process should address the risk of not being able to capitalize on unforeseen and previously unknown market opportunities, of not releasing product fast enough, of being subject to customer dissatisfaction e.g. by releasing untested version, the risk of releasing functions that are not what users expect or appreciate, the risk of lagging behind with regards to the competition.

Agile development is organized in a way that maximally mitigates that (business) risk. High-value needs are answered first. Product versions and updates are released quickly and frequently. They satisfy existing needs as well as include unexpected, innovative functions. They get users to pay for the product and optimize the stakeholders' return. They are of high quality in order to minimize maintenance and support and optimize the Total Cost of Ownership ('TCO').

Agile acknowledges the core purpose of the 'normal' IT activities (in figure 1.4 coarsely represented as Analyze, Design, Code and Test/Integrate), but breaks up their sequential organization. To produce releasable versions of product with the right dynamism and realize benefits sooner, the activities are structurally re-organized. The goal is to enable flexibility and speed instead of blocking them. In Agile all of these disciplines are performed in a non-linear, incremental way, concurrently and on a daily basis, by cross-skilled teams with continuous collaboration and negotiation about emergent ideas, techniques and practices.

The goal of such an integrated, cross-functional approach is to build-in quality and to prevent defects, rather than attempt to establish quality by a bug hunting approach in a post-creation phase. It is imperative to turn the desire to release regularly into the actual ability of doing so. Quality cannot be added to a finished product. Delays and budgets grow well out of hand when a lack of quality is identified after the actual creation process is over.

Aiming at the real and lasting benefits of Agile development requires going beyond the borders of the IT (or similarly technical) departments. The way that Agile not only embraces and incorporates change but even encourages it, is likely to challenge large parts of an organization. But it's more than a must; it is an *opportunity*. An entire organization will prosper from adopting the Agile way of working with its short cycles, frequent results and evolutionary adaptations. The Agile views and approach allow larger parts of organizations and departments to finally stop trying to predict the unpredictable. Agile incorporates dealing with answers, solutions and competing ideas that emerge *while* delivering product.

It might take some time to experience the fact that the continuous learning innate in Agile actually increases control amidst turbulent enterprise, business and market circumstances. It might take some time to shift management focus away from judgments over the past, e.g. via actuals and time registrations. It might take some time to gain confidence from optimizing and releasing business value through incremental outcomes of the Agile development process.

It might take some time to accept that agility takes time. It might take some time to accept that agility need not be analyzed, designed and planned before a transformation can take off.

■ 1.5   AGILITY CAN'T BE PLANNED

Agility is the *state* envisioned by moving to an Agile way of working. Agility is a state of continuous flux, high responsiveness, speed and adaptiveness. It is a state needed to deal with the unpredictability so common to the creative work that product development is and to the moving markets that organizations operate within.

Agility has no purpose if the aforementioned characteristics of flux, responsiveness, speed and adaptiveness are not expanded to the relationship of the organization and its markets, communities and consumers. The adoption of Agile processes is an important foundation for such full-scale *enterprise* agility. From the Agile adoption, new processes emerge, together with a new organizational culture of learning, improving and constant adaptation, and restored respect for people. Throughout the adoption important learnings are ingrained and injected into an organization's DNA.

There are some basic truths that are fundamental to setting the right expectations for any transformation toward a state of increased agility. Introducing Agile methods without accepting these essential truths closes the door to increased agility rather than turning it into a gateway of opportunities:

- Agility can't be planned;
- Agility can't be dictated;
- Agility can't be copied;
- Agility has no end-state.

A time-planned way to introduce Agile methods introduces awkward and unfavorable expectations. Introducing Agile methods is about introducing a new paradigm that will cause significant organizational turmoil. Existing procedures, departments and functions are impacted. The change is highly complex and therefore not predictable. In a transformation towards an Agile way of working, there is no way of predicting what needs of change will be encountered at what point in time, how these can be dealt with, how the new ways of working are being absorbed and what the exact outcome will be in order to plan and control the next steps. There is no way of predicting the pace at which the change will spread and take root.

Agility in itself is much more than following a new process. It is about behavior, it is about *cultural* change. A decision to move to Agile is a decision to leave the old (industrial) ways behind. It is not only about accepting but also celebrating the fact that agility is living the art of the possible. It requires the courage, honesty and determination of acting in the moment, acting upon the reality that is exposed by iterative-incremental progress information. Agility is about doing the best possible at every possible moment, constrained by the means we have and facing the constraints that arise. A time-planned way for an Agile transformation ignores the essence of Agile, that of dealing with complexity via well-considered steps of experimentation, learning and progress. Time-plans and trying to plan out agility against time constraints simply extend the old thinking. It is even counterproductive as a plan will actually slow down the transformation process, because serious delays and waiting times are incorporated.

Time-plans create the illusion of deadlines and a final end-state. Agility has no end-state. Agility is a state of continuous improvement, a state in which each status quo is challenged, by our own will or by external turbulence.

Agility is a unique and continuously evolving state that reflects the lessons and learnings that an organization went and goes through, the way in which specific annoyances and hindrances were overcome, the many inspections and adaptations that occurred along the journey. Agility is a unique signature, with imprints of the people, relationships, interactions, tools, processes, practices, constructs, within and across the many eco-systems that exist within an organization. No model can predict, outline or capture such a unique signature. Agility is a path requiring vision, belief, persistence and... hard work. Agility, as a state of high adaptability, is achieved by regularly adapting upon actual work producing observable results. What works today might not work tomorrow. What works for one combination of teams, technology and business might not work for another combination. Inspection without adaptation, in a world of complexity, creativity, fierce competition and unpredictability, is pointless. Adaptation without observation is direction-less.

Living the art of the possible against unpredicted outcomes engages people and accelerates a transformation as it shapes the future, thrives upon the unwritten state of the future and what that future might bring. It is a bright future for organizations that have the vision, the determination and the dedication; the courage to move away from following a plan or copying a model.

These basic truths must be in the hearts and minds of every person managing, guiding, facilitating or leading a transformation based on the Agile mindset. And even then, it still takes time for agility to settle in the hearts and minds of the people impacted by the transformation. After all, people have been instructed in wrong behavior through the industrial paradigm for a few decades, and often longer.

■ 1.6   COMBINING AGILE AND LEAN

For Lean, much like for Agile, it is vital to be aware that it's a set of thinking tools, a collection of interwoven principles that educate, motivate, value and guide people to continuously optimize their work and the way in which they work. The principles of Lean form the levers of a system that people can use to create better products faster, yet in a sustainable and respectful way. It's a system that rewards people for doing the best they can with the means and tools they are given in their actual situation.

There is not one definite, full-blown, one-size-fits-all, unified Lean process, for product development nor for manufacturing, with predefined and prescribed phases, roles, definitions, artifacts, deliverables, etc. A Lean process should be designed upon its underlying principles and thinking, and be constantly tuned to the actual situation. It's about adaptiveness. *The online 'Lean Primer' document of Bas Vodde and Craig Larman [Larman & Vodde, 2009] does an excellent job of introducing the roots of Lean along with its principles and thinking.*

1.6.1   Major aspects of Lean

People

The cornerstone of any system that claims to be Lean are the *people*. And 'people' refers to every possible actor in the whole ecosystem of a Lean product development/build system: customers, workers, teams, suppliers, and managers; internal and external.

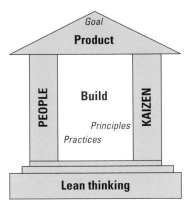

Figure 1.5 The temple of Lean

All people contribute in their own way and by their own means to manufacturing a product. They collaborate across skills to avoid hand-overs, delays and waiting times. They autonomously take decisions. They take the room to focus on knowledge gathering and constant learning. Managers act as teachers with a *go-see* commitment of workfloor presence. They promote the Lean thinking system; help people understand how to reflect on their work, their work results and how to build better products. The whole system embodies the spirit of *Kaizen*, the attitude of continuously thinking about the process, the product and possible improvements. Each member in the system can '*stop the line*'[2] if a problem occurs. The root of the problem will be identified, and countermeasures will be proposed or installed.

Everyone involved in the value chain works in an integrated way. Relationships with suppliers and external partners are not based upon the traditional approach of large volume purchases, big negotiation rounds and pressuring one another. It's all about building relationships on the mutual sharing of profit (and risk). Lean contracts incorporate mutual growth.

Waste

When considering the subject of waste, it is important that *avoiding* waste, via continuous improvement and small step optimizations, is the preferred option. Furthermore, 'waste' refers to process steps, not to people as an excuse to get rid of people.

Obviously, no matter how much attention is paid to avoiding it, waste can and will creep in. The Kaizen spirit drives all people to be committed, aware and critical in their daily work. It's a natural reflex.

A practice to identify structural waste is *Value Stream Mapping*. All steps and phases in the process of going from 'idea' to 'cash' are set out on a timeline. Activities may be labeled as 'valuable' or as 'non-value adding', but possibly also as necessary although not directly value-adding. The *Value Ratio* can be calculated as the ratio of time spent on value-adding activities versus wasteful activities. It's a figure that may serve as a baseline against which improvement can be measured. But, as in all improvement activities, there is no definite end goal, no final state. The improvement itself is the goal.

Inventory, WIP and flow

Lean strives for continuity and flow. Overproduction and excessive inventory disrupt flow and may delay the discovery and resolution of quality issues. But it is also disrespectful as it forces people to do work that may actually never be used. Inventory is costly and makes an organization liable to waste.

Lean says to limit 'Work in Process' (and costly inventory) by producing only materials to be used further down the line in a 'Just in Time' mode, i.e. when there is a *pull* signal from the next steps in the process. A *kanban* is a physical signal card for this function in manufacturing systems. A kanban is attached to an inventory of parts. It is linked to a level of stock. New parts are only produced when enough materials have been used and the signal card appears.

1.6.2   Implementing Lean

Much like with Agile, many organizations struggle with Lean. And on top of that, organizations struggle with the combination of Agile and Lean.

In general, companies refer to organizational problems when expressing a desire for 'Lean'. If they want to become 'Agile' on the other hand, they are most likely referring to problems with product development. However, neither Agile nor Lean offer one magical, off-the-shelf (silver bullet) solution.

Unfortunately, Lean is far too frequently limited to *eliminate waste*. Just picking out that one element from the toolbox is already an undesirable over-focus on just one aspect, instead of looking at the whole. It gets even worse when the principle itself is broken, and when 'elimination' is applied to (get rid of) *people* and not as a means to improve *processes and structures*. The highly popular management sport of 'cost cutting' tends to twist this important Lean practice into designating people's work as 'overhead', i.e. non-valuable. The underlying signal is that the people who are doing that work are waste and... disposable.

From that popular misconception and its all too limited perspective on Lean, it is a long journey to build up an understanding that Lean is primarily about respecting people in order to optimize value and quality. That Lean is more about the *context* in which people can prosper in order to perform, than about continuously over-stressing the need for results and performance. It invokes the difficult exercise of replacing 'command and control', big boss behavior, micro-management, over-allocation and nano-assignments with decentralized decision-making mechanisms.

It is a long way from this misconception to an understanding of Lean beyond the formal practices, an understanding of Lean as a thinking context with no definite end state, with people continuously reflecting on their daily work and self-improving.

Agile helps.

There are more than just a few similarities between Agile and Lean that are worthwhile exploring. Some management or governance philosophies should not be mixed because this will result in a blurry amalgam and the unique flavor of the ingredients will get lost in the mix, as will the benefits. But, as far as Agile and Lean are concerned, I don't only believe that Lean and Agile *can* be combined, the combination of Lean management principles with Agile product development thinking, as a total outcome, will actually result in a more powerful mix.

Lean and Agile are truly *blending* philosophies. Lean thrives on a powerful but typical mindset. Agile has distinct views that not only match the main Lean principles extremely well, but even form a very tangible implementation of them for product delivery purposes.

1.6.3   The blending philosophies of Lean and Agile

'The Blending Philosophies of Lean and Agile' is also the title of a more detailed paper I have published on this subject [Verheyen, 2011]. Here I introduce just some of the clear strategies in Agile that align it with Lean:

- *Potentially unused inventories:* Detailed requirements, hard-coded plans, designs, etc. form a liability in software and other forms of complex product development, and not an asset, because they represent potentially unused work. Agile avoids producing these upfront in every possible detail. If the potential point of implementation of identified work is still some time away, the chances are considerable that this work will not be performed. The exact expectations may change in the meantime, or experience from intermediate implementation and releases may indicate better ways of doing the distant work. Only the upcoming, highest ordered work is detailed more, as this is what will be worked on next. And even then, a team will only *pull* in the amount of work they deem feasible for an iteration, and start building it based on progressive learning and continuous improvement, even on a daily basis.

- *Partially done work:* Work that is not completely finished, 'almost there, I just need a little more time'-type of work, is a known, important type of waste. In an Agile process the goal of each iteration is to produce a *working* piece of product. No unfinished work is included in the observable result. The overall Kaizen thinking, and its explicit daily *Inspect & Adapt* implementation in Agile, helps teams in not taking up new work while undone work remains in the iteration. Time-boxing is a time-management technique that helps teams focus on finishing work.

- *Feature usage*: Research has shown that barely 20% of the features included in a (software) product built in a traditional way are regularly used [Standish, 2002; Standish 2013]. Unused or under-used functions thus represent an enormous waste of effort and budget, both in terms of developing as well as in maintaining them. Active collaboration with people who know and represent the customers and users prevents the production of unwanted or non-valuable requirements, and helps a team focus on minimal sets of features that may actually be appreciated. The focus on 'wanted' requirements saves not only development budget, it also ensures that future maintenance and support costs can be kept much lower. And the iterative-incremental process allows teams to regularly adapt the product based upon an effective appreciation of the delivered value and also capitalize on new value opportunities.

Agile has clear strategies for continuous improvement, thereby leveraging the Kaizen spirit:

- The work plan of an Agile team is checked and updated daily;
- At the end of an iteration the product version (whether released or in a state of being releasable) is verified to gather feedback, remarks, improvements and enhancements;
- The process, the way the teams work, collaborate, communicate and undertake implementation, is verified at its latest point via an iteration retrospective.

Agile *optimizes the whole* by demanding that customers or their proxies express and order work, and take an active part in the development process for clarification and functional trade-offs, even during implementation. All implementation skills are available within a team to turn ideas, options and requirements into working versions in a single iteration, or less.

Agile shortens cycle times by optimizing the value stream through the prevention of traditional waiting activities like hand-overs and external decisions. There are no macro hand-overs, i.e. hand-overs across departments and organizations, which typically occur in a sequential organization of work with large blocks of specialized work packages. But there are also no micro hand-overs, i.e. hand-overs between individuals within a team, given the collective accountability of the team.

In general, the strategies and principles of Agile are consistent with, and even leveraging, all major Lean principles, as indicated in the following representation:

Lean	Agile
Respect for People	Self-organizing Teams
Kaizen	Inspect & adapt, short feedback cycles
Prevent/eliminate Waste	No unused specs, architecture or infrastructure
Pull inventory (Kanban)	Estimates and planned work reflect team capacity
Visual management	Information radiators
Built-in Quality	Definition of Done, Development standards
Customer Value	Active Business Collaboration
Optimizing the whole	Whole Team Together (incl. stakeholders)
Deliver fast	Timeboxed iterations and working Increments
The manager-teacher	The facilitating servant-leader

Figure 1.6 The consistency in principles of Lean and Agile

1 Frederick Taylor (1856-1915) was an American engineer who is best known for his research into ways to optimize the productivity, efficiency and the cost of labor. He promoted enforced standardization and the enforced adoption of systematic methods and practices. Control lay exclusively with management, with workers being there only to carry out the work.
2 This refers to the Toyota car manufacturing origins of Lean, where every person at the production line is entitled to stop the line when problems, defects or a lack of quality are detected.

2 Scrum

■ 2.1 THE HOUSE OF SCRUM

The house of Scrum is a warm house. It's a house where people are
W E L C O M E.

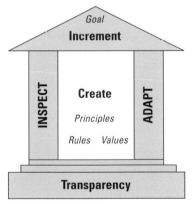

Figure 2.1 The house of Scrum

In the house of Scrum people from different backgrounds, in different roles,
with different skills, talents and personalities work, learn and improve
together. The house of Scrum is an inclusive house of warm, open and
collaborative relationships.

The house of Scrum knows no 'versus'. Barriers are removed, instead of being maintained or created. There's no business versus IT in the house of Scrum, no team versus the world, no Product Owner versus Development Team, no coding versus supporting, no testers versus programmers, no 'my' team versus 'your' team, no Scrum Master versus the organization. The house of Scrum offers an open view on the world. The house of Scrum is a great and energizing place where product development prospers from the combined, creative intelligence of self-organizing people.

The house of Scrum helps to stay away from rigid behavior and rigid structures. The inhabitants of the house of Scrum, their teams and the ecosystems in which they operate show flexibility to better deal with uncertainty, internal tensions within and external pressure on the ecosystem. They probe, sense and adapt at all levels; at strategic and tactical levels, from requirements to plans to objectives to markets to technology.

Scrum is an enabler for delivering products better and faster. But, most of all, energy and work pleasure are restored for all the involved players; from those who create the products, to those who have a stakeholder interest in the product, to those who consume the product and its services, to all those who co-create it with opinions, feedback and appreciation. The workplace is humanized through Scrum.

■ 2.2   SCRUM, WHAT'S IN A NAME?

The term 'Scrum' was first used by Hirotaka Takeuchi and Ikujiro Nonaka, two acknowledged management thinkers, in their ground-breaking 1986 paper *'The New New Product Development Game'* [Takeuchi & Nonaka, 1986].

With the term 'Scrum' they referred in their paper to the game of rugby to stress the importance of team work and some analogies between a team sport like rugby and being successful in the game of new product development. The research described in their paper showed that out-standing performance in the development of new, complex products is achieved when teams, as small and self-organizing units of people, are given objectives, not tasks. The best performing teams are those that are given direction within which they have room to devise their own tactics on how to best head towards their joint objective. Teams require autonomy to achieve excellence.

... as in Rugby, the ball gets passed within the team as it moves as a unit up the field.
Takeuchi Nonaka (1986).
The New New Product Development Game

Figure 2.2 A Scrum in the game of rugby

Jeff Sutherland and Ken Schwaber conceived the Scrum process for Agile software development in the early 90's. They presented Scrum for the first time in 1995 at the Oopsla[1] conference in Austin, Texas (US) [Schwaber, 1995; Sutherland, 1995].

They inherited the name 'Scrum' from the paper by Takeuchi and Nonaka. The Scrum framework implements the principles described in this paper for developing and sustaining complex products. If teams are only instructed to carry out executable tasks and their capacity in hours is pre-filled with such tasks, team members suffer from a narrowed mind. They are restricted from looking and thinking beyond the instructions, even if reality or experience shows that the prescribed solution is difficult to achieve or is suboptimal. They lose openness for better solutions, for solutions that are not dictated but are a better fit to the actual demand given changes, proven findings and current circumstances. Their only focus is to produce what was instructed without considering conflicting ideas and options, without dealing with the natural instability typical to product development and technological discovery. The industrial mode to direct people as if they were robots impedes building on the collective intelligence of a team, thereby upfront limiting their work results to mediocre levels.

The remarkable similarities between Lean and Agile were pointed out in section 1.6. There is also a connection between Scrum and Lean via 'The New New Product Development Game', and the term 'Scrum'.

The authors of the 'The New New Product Development Game' paper are very familiar with, and are proponents of, Lean. Over the course of their careers and assignments they have studied and described well-known Lean companies. Yet, they never use the term 'Lean'.

In their paper, Takeuchi and Nonaka chose to describe the beating heart of Lean, and called it 'Scrum', as a differentiator in terms of complex product development. The viewpoint is that an organization is unlikely to benefit from any so-called 'Lean' practice for developing complex products if this beating heart (Scrum) is not present and only the practices surrounding it are installed. As this is the case for many Lean implementations, the authors preferred to stress the need for the heart and soul of the system and take away the focus on the surrounding management practices.

So, they don't mention Lean, and focus instead on its essential engine, Scrum. Furthermore, they barely talk about 'Lean' because it became synonymous with just the *management* practices of the Toyota Production System.

"Scrum should be at the heart of every implementation of Lean." [Sutherland, 2011]

■ 2.3   IS THAT A GORILLA I SEE OVER THERE?

Evolutionary practices for software development have been around
for a long time [Larman, 2004]. The Scrum process for Agile software
development is available and documented since 1995. The Agile movement
was formed in 2001 [Beck, et.al., 2001]. This new paradigm for the software
industry quickly took root and its adoption has been increasing steadily.

A widely accepted model to assess and represent the degree of adoption of a
technological product or service is Geoffrey Moore's 'Technology Adoption
Life Cycle' (TALC) [Moore, 1999; Wiefels, 2002].

Geoffrey Moore based his adapted model on the difference observed in
the adoption pattern for *technology* products or services representing a
disruptive new paradigm, a paradigm causing an important discontinuity
in innovation. Moore confirmed the general phases and audiences to be in
line with the more traditional adoption of products representing a more
continuous evolution. But after the phase of *Early Market*, Moore observed,
and added to the model, a period of stagnation. It is a period where
adoption stalls. An unpredictable time passes by before entering the next
phase of adoption, the *Bowling Alley*. Some products never even get out of
this stand-still and simply disappear. Moore called this period the *Chasm*.

During the highly turbulent phase of the *Bowling Alley* a *gorilla* is formed,
a market leader. In the subsequent phases, until the disappearance of the
product from the market, gorilla-market leaders are difficult to overthrow.

In addition to the use of Agile for the delivery of new, possibly disruptive,
technological products, Agile in itself is a new, and clearly disruptive,
paradigm on the technology market.

The years since the emergence of the first Agile processes (*avant la lettre*)
and the official establishment of the term 'Agile' in 2001 marked the *Early
Market* phase of the Agile paradigm.

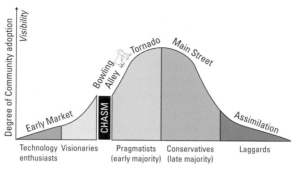

Figure 2.3 The Technology Adoption Life Cycle

Around 2007 Agile was crossing the Chasm. Up to that point, evidence on Agile was mostly anecdotal and generally based on individual enterprise adoptions, isolated cases and personal storytelling. This is typical for these phases of the technology adoption life cycle. It is equally typical that mostly enthusiasts and visionaries were attracted by it. But once the Chasm was crossed, Agile also became attractive to a broader audience, the audience of early majority-Pragmatists. They typically look at the business advantages of a less proven paradigm and compare its problem-solving capabilities to the existing paradigm. Yahoo! is an important example of a large company transitioning to Agile in those years, and documenting their experiences in 2008 [Benefield, 2008].

In Q3 2009, Forrester Research and Dr. Dobb's [Hammond & West, 2009] conducted a survey amongst IT professionals worldwide including an investigation into the type of "methodology (that) most closely reflects the development process you are currently using". Perhaps surprisingly, 36% of the participants indicated that they were doing Agile, while only 13% confirmed to be following a waterfall process[2]. This confirmed the common perception that the use of Agile had indeed gradually been overtaking the waterfall model, and that Agile had crossed the chasm.

In April 2012, Forrester Research [Giudice, 2011] published the results of a
survey on the global adoption of Agile for software application development
noting that "the IT industry is (...) widely adopting Agile" and that the
adoption of Agile was not limited to small enterprises. Large organizations
form a substantial part of the companies moving to Agile. Forrester also
found that "Shorter iterations and Scrum practices are the most common
Agile practices" and confirmed the widespread finding that Scrum is the
most commonly applied method for Agile software development. Forrester
thereby validated the results of the yearly 'State of Agile Development'
surveys conducted by VersionOne [VersionOne, 2011; VersionOne, 2013].

Although the adoption of Scrum is not typical or limited to a specific
economic sector, Forrester found the financial services industry to show a
remarkably high adoption degree of Agile methods. This is striking as large
financial institutions are by their nature very risk averse. In the aftermath of
the global financial crisis of 2008, it seems that many began adopting Scrum
successfully as I could document for a large financial organization in the
Netherlands in 2012 [Verheyen & Arooni, 2012].

The post-Chasm years of Agile show many back-and-forth movements,
preventing us from clearly distinguishing the Bowling Alley from
the Tornado yet. The post-Chasm years of Agile are marked by a
strong whirlwind, with Scrum as a stable anchor and reference though.

Inside of the whirlwind, three waves of Scrum have manifested.

■ The first wave of Scrum was mostly a reconnaissance wave.
  Organizations found that the old, industrial ways no longer sufficed
  to solve, or even patch, the problems in their IT and software delivery
  domains. Scrum was adopted as the new IT delivery process.
■ During the second wave of Scrum, large organizations discovered they
  were at the end of the old ways of working too. As Scrum entered this
  new market segment, 'scale' and divergence became the dominant

themes. Although Scrum's terminology was everywhere, sub-groups and derivative movements took off. New names, movements and methods were invented, introduced, launched, and often disbanded again.

- The third Scrum Wave is fueled by a desire for simplicity. Organizations discover that fighting complexity with complexity is not helping. Too much waste, organizational complexity and fundamental impediments remain unresolved by the (often complex) solutions of the second wave. Organizations renew their acquaintance with Scrum. They start appreciating that Scrum is well-defined and clearly stated, yet establishes a frame that leaves much room for diversity. They start understanding how Scrum can wrap a variety of strategies and techniques within the boundaries of inspection and adaptation created.

While Scrum enters many non-software domains of society, convergence appears on the horizon, where the whirlwind might start calming down. Agile professionals worldwide sow seeds, and fertilize the grounds for many organizations to start bearing fruits of their adoption of Scrum,

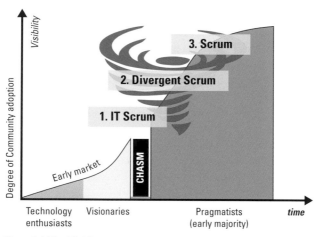

Figure 2.4 The third Scrum wave

the point where they start enacting Scrum. Scrum is affirmed as the dominant definition of Agile post-Chasm.

> Scrum is the de facto standard against which to measure, to oppose or to join. Scrum has emerged as the gorilla of the Agile family of methods.

■ 2.4   FRAMEWORK, NOT METHODOLOGY

Scrum, with its roots in new product development theory, is designed to help teams create, deliver and sustain complex products in turbulent circumstances via self-organization. Scrum implements the scientific method of empiricism to better deal with complexity and unpredictability. Scrum replaces the industrial, plan-driven approach with well-considered, opportunistic experimentation. The definition of the Scrum framework has been consciously limited to a bare minimal set of mandatory elements, making each element essential. Breaking Scrum's base design by leaving out one or more elements is likely to cover up problems, instead of revealing them.

The purpose of empiricism via Scrum is to help people perform inspections & adaptations upon transparency of the work being undertaken and results being produced. Scrum foresees frequent reality checks to assure the best possible decisions. Scrum helps to adjust, adapt, change and gain flexibility. The rules, principles and values of the framework, as described in the Scrum Guide [Schwaber & Sutherland, 2017], serve this purpose.

Scrum, through its minimalistic design, has no exhaustive and formal prescriptions on how to design and plan the behavior of all actors, nor does it lay out their expected behavior against time, let alone how the work must be documented, maintained and stored. Scrum has no rules for upfront instructions of document types and deliverables to be produced. Neither does Scrum instruct the exact time of their production. Instead of installing, thriving and relying on hand-overs, toll gates and control meetings, Scrum exposes them as a major source of delays, waste and disrespect, leaving it up to the organization to de-install them (or not).

Methodologies, by design, are composed of stringent and mandatory sequences of steps, processes and procedures, implementing predefined algorithms and executers for each step, process or procedure. This holds the promise of success when the prescriptions are followed. As such, 'methodologies' aspire to replace the creativity, autonomy and intellectual powers of people with components like phases, tasks, must-do practices and patterns, executable techniques and tools. Practice and research show that obedience to a methodology in a cognitive environment only serves to ensure formal coverage for blame, not the success of working results. Methodologies depend on high degrees of predictability to have a high yield. Complex product development does not have that high degree of predictability. It is even more unpredictable than it is predictable.

Scrum is the opposite of such a big collection of interwoven mandatory components and maximal set of complete prescriptions. Scrum is not a methodology. Scrum replaces a pre-programmed algorithmic approach with a heuristic one, with respect for people and self-organization in order to deal with unpredictability and to address complex problems.

If and when Scrum is referred to as a 'process', it is certainly not a process of the repeatable kind. That is a challenge to explain, in the sense that the term 'process' typically invokes a sense of algorithmic and predictable steps, repeatable actions and enforceable top-down control; the sort of expectations that are typical for... a methodology.

If referred to as a 'process', then Scrum is a *servant* process, not a *commanding* process. What works best for all involved players and their processes at work, emerges from the use of Scrum, not from a dictate by Scrum's definition. Players discover the work required to close the gap between an observable intermediate result and an envisioned outcome, where the intermediate result inhibits the characteristics of the envisioned final result. Scrum is a process that helps surface the most effective process, practices and structures. Scrum creates the boundaries to help discover a way of working that is continuously adaptable to everybody's actual context and current circumstances. Scrum is… a framework.

> The framework of Scrum sets the bounded environments for action, and leaves it to the people to take action, thereby deciding themselves what the best possible action is within those boundaries.

■ 2.5 PLAYING THE GAME

Scrum, as a *framework* for Agile development, was designed to optimize and control the creation of *valuable* products in turbulent enterprise, organizational, business and market circumstances.

Figure 2.5 The Scrum game board

The game board of Scrum shows the essential elements and principles of Scrum, everything that is required to play the game.

Scrum requires much discipline from its players, while leaving plenty of room for personal creativity and context-specific tactics. The rules of the game are based upon respect for the people-players through a subtle and balanced distribution of accountability. Respecting the rules of the game, not taking shortcuts on rules and roles, nor short-circuiting the empirical grounds of the game, delivers the most joys and greatest benefits for the players as well as in terms of results.

The Scrum game board shows the players, the artifacts, the events and the main principles of the game of Scrum. The rules of Scrum bind these elements together.

2.5.1 Players and accountabilities

Agile methods are driven by a sense of business opportunism. The time-management technique of time-boxing all work allows the players to quickly respond to new opportunities and adapt to any changes and evolutions.

Scrum organizes its players around three peer accountabilities, each complementing the other ones, thereby turning collaboration into the key to success:

- Product Owner;
- Development Team;
- Scrum Master.

Product Owner is a one-person player role injecting the business perspective of the product into the delivery process. A Product Owner represents all stakeholders, internal and external, to the *Development Team*, a multi person player role. Although a Product Owner may have strategic product management tasks beyond the Scrum Team, it is important that the Product

Owner actively engages with the other players of the team regularly and repeatedly.

The Product Owner assures with the Development Team that a *Product Backlog* exists. The Product Owner manages the Product Backlog based on the product vision as a long-term view of the road ahead. A Product vision captures *why* the product exists.

The Product Backlog shows all of the work actually envisioned for the product that's being created and sustained. This work may comprise functional and non-functional expectations, enhancements, fixes, patches, ideas, updates and other requirements. If anybody wants to know what work is identified and planned for the product they only have to look at the Product Backlog.

The Product Owner expresses the business expectations and ideas captured in the Product Backlog to the team and orders the items in the Product Backlog to optimize the value delivered. The Product Owner manages the game budget to optimize the balance of value, effort and time for the represented stakeholders.

The *Development Team* self-organizes to perform all end-to-end development activities required to turn items from the Product Backlog, expressed and ordered by the Product Owner, into releasable versions of product. 'Development' applies to all work undertaken by the Development Team within a Sprint. Depending on the context it might include the creation of test cases, testing activities, programming, documentation, integration, release activities, etc. It covers all work necessary to guarantee that the *Increment* of product is in a usable state no later than by the end of a Sprint, and that it technically can be released to the users and consumers of the product or service. That state of the Increment is called 'Done'. The qualities and criteria that need to be met to reach that state, also driving the development work to be undertaken by the Development Team, are captured in a 'definition of Done'.

The Development Team has a set of 'Development Standards' to describe how the implementation is being performed. This is required to guarantee the level of quality needed to release regularly. And it provides the right transparency to the way the game is being played.

The Development Team sets the cost or effort indication on Product Backlog items. The Development Team selects the amount of work it assumes it can handle in a Sprint at the start of that particular Sprint. The evolving effort indications on Product Backlog can be compared with proven experience to make a *forecast* of Product Backlog for a Sprint.

Scrum Master is a one-person player role to facilitate the Product Owner and the Development Team, within the organization, during the game. A Scrum Master teaches, coaches and mentors the team and the organization, in understanding, respecting and knowing how to play the game of Scrum. The Scrum Master makes sure the rules of the game are well understood and that any elements that hinder or block the team in its progress are removed. Such elements are called *Impediments* in Scrum.

The Scrum Master induces the continual desire to become better players. The Scrum Master implements Scrum by helping others make better use of Scrum.

2.5.2   Time
The time-boxed iterations in the game of Scrum are called *Sprints*. Sprints allow the Development Team to focus on achieving the next game level, the *Sprint Goal*, with minimal external disruptions.

All work in Scrum is organized in Sprints. Scrum has no typecasted Sprints as the goal of *each* Sprint is to deliver a valuable piece of working product, a (product) *Increment*. A Sprint's duration is never more than four weeks and typically takes one to four weeks.

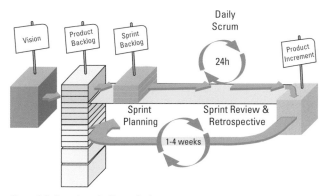

Figure 2.6 Overview of a Scrum Sprint

As a container event, the Sprint encapsulates the other Scrum events. Every event is time-boxed and is an opportunity to change course or adapt to changing conditions:

- Sprint Planning;
- Daily Scrum;
- Sprint Review;
- Sprint Retrospective.

Every Sprint begins with *Sprint Planning* where the Development Team pulls work into the Sprint from the current Product Backlog. The team selects the amount of work it deems feasible for the Sprint against the expectations of what it takes to make it releasable. The selected work is a *forecast* that represents the insights that the team has at the time of selection. The Development Team might look at the amount of work they have, on average, completed in past Sprints and compare this to their capacity for the upcoming Sprint, to slightly increase the accuracy of the forecast. The views of the Product Owner are respected, and additional details are discussed with the Product Owner.

The selected work, the forecast, is designed, analyzed and elaborated into an actionable work plan for the time-boxed Sprint, the *Sprint Backlog*. After the expiration of the time-box of Sprint Planning, or possibly sooner, the Development Team starts to work upon this plan that has been collaboratively created. Sprint Planning never takes more than eight hours.

To manage and follow up on its development work the Development Team organizes a short, 15 minutes, daily event called the *Daily Scrum.* It is a right-time planning event. The plan of the upcoming work of the team is optimized for achieving the Sprint Goal based upon the actual progress within the Sprint. The adaptation is captured in an update of the Sprint Backlog. The actual progress on the Sprint Backlog is visualized, based upon the amount of remaining work. If the actual progress impacts the forecast, the Development Team consults with the Product Owner.

As the Sprint progresses, an Increment of the product emerges from the team's collaborative work. If the Product Owner, as sole representative of all stakeholders, deems the Increment useful then the Increment can be released without delay. At the end of the Sprint, the Increment is inspected in a *Sprint Review;* to check on the functional fitness to release it or the actual usage if already released.

The Product Owner maintains a high level of transparency by presenting Product Backlog evolutions against the long-term product vision at the Sprint Review. While reviewing the product Increment all players are likely to discover changes and receive feedback and evolutionary insights from the inspection. These are processed into the Product Backlog for future implementation, while understanding that the exact implementation date depends on the Product Owner's ordering and the team's sustainable progress. Sprint Review never takes more than four hours.

The Sprint is concluded with a Sprint Retrospective in which the Scrum Team inspects, and reflects upon, the complete, *well*, 'process'. The event covers all aspects of the work, i.e. release suitability of the product, technology, social aspects, the Scrum process, development practices, collaboration, product quality, etc. The event is basically about establishing what went well, where there is room for improvement and what experiments might be usefully conducted in order to learn and build a better product.

As part of continuous improvement, the Scrum Team agrees on pre-servations, adjustments, experiments and improvements for the next Sprint. A Sprint Retrospective never takes more than three hours.

> Scrum only knows Sprints, and the goal of each Sprint is to deliver a version of working product, an Increment of the product. Working versions of product are considered the only measure of progress.

Sprint length is kept steady over several Sprints for reasons of cadence. It is the heartbeat of development and it's useful for the team to understand how much work can be done during a Sprint.

The amount of work that could be done in a Sprint is sometimes called *Velocity*. Velocity is an indication of the amount of work a team was able to create in past Sprints. Velocity is the sum of effort or cost units that were completed in a Sprint and is typical to one team, and one team's composition.

The Sprint length is right-sized to capitalize on emerging and previously unforeseen business opportunities. The collaborative Sprint Review provides the Product Owner with the best possible information on how additional Sprints can further improve the value of the product, taking into account a balance of risk, effort, budget and cohesion.

The Sprint length may also depend on how long a team can work without consulting with stakeholders at the Sprint Review. The Sprint Review is an opportunity to adapt to new strategic or market directions.

A team will suffer from reduced learning and adaptation opportunities when not consulting with stakeholders, and knowing of markets, business evolutions and new strategies at least every four weeks. Sprints may be shorter than four weeks, but never longer.

2.5.3   Tracking progress

Overall progress of work is tracked and visualized, in order to know about progress *trends* for forecasting purposes, looking into the uncertain future based upon the proven, and observable past.

In order to continuously measure and adapt to reality and achieve the best forecasts possible, always taking complexity into account, the remaining work is re-estimated regularly and honestly:

- *Sprint progress:* Within a Sprint, progress is tracked on a daily basis. The Sprint Backlog always holds the most accurate, realistic plan for the work remaining to implement the Sprint Goal.
- *Product progress:* The progress indication at the level of the Product Backlog is updated and reviewed at a minimum at the Sprint Review. The Product Owner may package Product Backlog items and Increments into tentative releases. The proven progress of past Sprints gives the Product Owner and its stakeholders a forecasted delivery date for releases, individual features or feature sets.

The classic Scrum approach to visualize progress is a *Burn-down chart*, a graph showing the evolution of total remaining work:

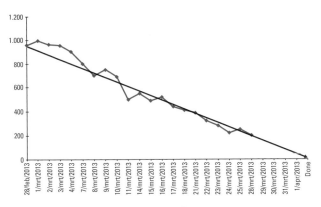

Figure 2.7 Example of a Sprint Burn-down chart

However, the team decides on the best way to represent progress. This may be a burn-down chart, a physical Scrum board, a burn-up chart (e.g. in value), or it could be a cumulative flow diagram to better visualize the flow of work:

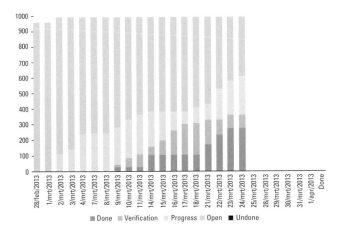

Figure 2.8 Example of a Cumulative Flow Diagram

2.5.4   The value of the Product Backlog

The value of the Product Backlog lies not in completeness, precision, detail or perfection, nor in capturing every possible requirement in every possible detail against every possible timing horizon. The value of the Product Backlog lies in transparency, in making clear what work needs to be done in order to create a minimally viable and valuable product (or product Increment). The Product Backlog brings out into the open all work, development, compliances, and constraints that a team has to deal with in order to create releasable versions of product.

Product Backlog is an ordered list of ideas, features and options to bring an envisioned product to life, to deliver it and subsequently sustain and grow it. The list is bound to include all functionalities and features, but naturally also includes fixes, maintenance work, architectural work, work to be spent on security, scalability, stability and performance, etc. At the time of the creation of an item on the Product Backlog, the item is supposedly valuable for a customer or contributing to the ability to add value.

Every item on the Product Backlog holds just enough detail to make clear what value it represents. An item is intentionally incomplete to encourage additional and explicit discussion over it. Each Product Backlog item serves as a placeholder for discussion at the appropriate time.

The Product Owner has accountability over the Product Backlog. A Product Owner however will still take into account the technical and development input from the Development Team. A Product Owner however will still take into account dependencies, non-functional requirements and organizational expectations.

The Product Backlog is gradually refined, thereby introducing incremental management of the product requirements:

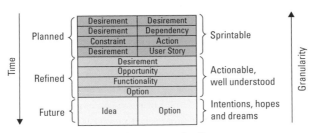

Figure 2.9 Incremental evolution of Product Backlog

As development progresses, Product Backlog is refined, adjusted and updated. Product Backlog is continuously ordered and re-ordered by the Product Owner. The items are regularly refined in conjunction with the Development Team. Product Backlog is a living artifact.

The Product Owner looks to balance the needs of all stakeholders, internal and external, who are to be represented to the Scrum Team. Continuously adhering to 'just enough' descriptions and designs of the work, i.e. leaving out unnecessary details, ensures that no excessive money and time is wasted if the item ultimately isn't created or is implemented much later or in a different fashion.

The level of description and detail of a Product Backlog item lies somewhere between what is a desire and what used to be a requirement. A 'desire' is too fuzzy to work on and a (traditional) 'requirement' is over-specified and over-detailed. Over-specification in development impedes the optimal use of technology, blocks the ability to capitalize on synergies between different functions and is a waste of money in situations of even minimal turbulence or change. Therefore, the term 'desirement' is well suited to describe the granularity of a Product Backlog item.

Desirements move in their ordering from Product Backlog via Sprint Backlog into Increments of working product. While the ordering of the

Product Backlog depends upon a complex combination of factors like cost/ effort, dependencies, priority, cohesion and consistency, it is essential to also have a view on the assumed value of a Product Backlog item.

Core factors for a Product Backlog item are cost and value:
- *Cost:* The cost, or effort, of a Product Backlog item is generally expressed in a relative unit. Past Sprints show a team how much work, expressed in the chosen unit, can be converted on average into a working Increment during a Sprint. Upon this empirical given, an expectation can be created of when an item on the actual Product Backlog might become available as part of an evolving product. It is a forecast, not moving the players into the realm of exact predictions, understanding that any such expectation is constrained by today's knowledge and circumstances.
- Value: An important principle of Agile is "to satisfy the customer through early and continuous delivery of valuable software." [Beck, et.al., 2001] Without an attribute for (business) value on Product Backlog items, a Product Owner has no idea of how much value a feature, an idea or a feature set presumably brings to the customer whom he/she represents within the Scrum Team. Value will depend on the type of enterprise, the type of product and its market. The value of a Product Backlog item can be indirect, in it that not picking up a Product Backlog item might undercut the value of the system or even the organization, or that not ordering it high on the Product Backlog may produce negative value, or undermine the future ability to create value.

The notion of value helps Product Owners and their stakeholders move away from the (false idea of) perfection of a total product that must be completely built before even considering its release. The focus shifts to a minimal marketable product release and the minimal work it takes to effectively bring value to the marketplace. Product Backlog can be used to group items, features and non-functional requirements into cohesive feature sets.

Product Backlog is all the plan Scrum requires, its 'desirements' hold all the information to make forecasts about scope and time, if needed. A Product Backlog item needs the right attributes to be ordered, more than just being prioritized.

2.5.5 The importance of Done

In a definition of 'Done' the qualities and criteria are expressed that need to be met by an Increment of product in order for it to be 'releasable', to be able to release it into production. The definition of Done holds the product qualities and -often- the activities, criteria, tasks and work that need to be performed on a working piece of product for it to be of production quality. "Done" is a quality of the Increment and is therefore part of the Scrum artifacts.

The definition of Done is essential to understand and plan the work needed to create a releasable Increment at Sprint Planning and for the inspection of that Increment at the Sprint Review. The definition of Done serves the transparency required in Scrum in terms of the work to be done and the work actually done.

The prefix 'potentially' is, however, added to 'releasable Increment'. This refers to the Product Owner's accountability to decide upon the actual release of an Increment; a decision that will likely be based on business cohesion and functional usefulness as observed during the Sprint or at the Sprint Review. Yet, the Product Owner's release decision should not be constrained by 'development' work, hence all work required to achieve the level of Done is performed no later than before the Sprint Review in the Sprint.

The empiricism of Scrum only functions well with transparency. Transparency requires common standards to work against and to inspect upon. The definition of Done sets the standard for *releasable* and should be known by all players. Transparency means not only visible, but also understandable. The content of the definition of Done should be self-explanatory.

An organization that thrives and depends on products and services can be expected to have a definition of product qualities in place, and to express such through standards, guidelines, rules, service levels and other expectations. A professional organization defines quality. Scrum Development Teams, consisting of professional product developers, are an integral part of an organization, rather than being isolated gangs of thug coders within the organization. Such Development Teams can be expected to adhere to the overarching product standards as set by the organization.

If, as can be expected, the minimal definition of Done is provided by the organization, a Development Team will still complement it with context-specific elements; the product, a release or technology. In the absence of such organizational guidelines, a Development Team should, as professionals, create an appropriate definition of Done for their work.

Through an agreed definition of Done, quality is at the heart of Scrum. No undone work is part of an Increment. No undone work is put into production. *Ever.* From the inspection of the Increment based upon the definition of Done, the collaborative conversation at the Sprint Review might include quality, and requirements with regards to the definition of quality in the organization. This helps the team consider the appropriateness of the definition of Done at the subsequent Sprint Retrospective. The self-organizing drive of the Development Team will make them include all that is actually possible, and more, while taking into account the feedback from the stakeholders.

Primary ownership of the definition of Done lies with the Development Team, in the same way that primary ownership of Product Backlog lies with the Product Owner. The Development Team is accountable for the hard work related to delivering working versions of product that comply to the definition of Done. A definition of Done can't be cut short by forces outside of the Development Team. The Development Team will build upon general, organizational expectations and definitions (including the development, engineering, quality or operations areas). The Development Team will add product-specific qualities and will obviously incorporate the functional or business quality expectations from the Product Owner.

Decisions over the definition of Done might depend on the presence of skills, authorizations and availability of systems, services and interfaces. Although dependencies on external systems or interfaces might lead to re-ordering of the work on the Product Backlog, a Development Team prefers to make progress. A team can use stubs, mock-ups or simulators for non-available systems or non-resolved technical dependencies. But all parties remain aware that the work is not really Done, as the definition of Done does not reflect releasable. It increases the independence of the team but does not remove the dependence. There is an unpredictable amount of work hidden in the system and it must be performed at some point in order to actually release the product. In the meantime, the Product Owner is blocked from making that decision. Fortunately, the Sprint Review ultimately reveals this information to stakeholders too, so the chances are bigger that appropriate actions will be taken within the organization.

The definition of Done stresses the importance of seizing the opportunity to release by doing all of the work required to capitalize on an opportunity within a Sprint.

■ 2.6   CORE PRINCIPLES OF SCRUM

The Scrum game board in figure 2.5 not only shows the formally mandatory elements of Scrum but also three main principles underlying Scrum:

- Shared (visual) workspace;
- Self-organization;
- Empiricism (aka 'empirical process control').

2.6.1   Shared (visual) workspace

Teams, in order to function properly and grow in terms of effectiveness and performance, need a shared workspace for their interactions and collaboration. The team organizes its own workspace to optimize dialogue, communication and collaboration. This includes removing barriers - physical or mental - that obstruct the flow of information. The shared workspace facilitates the team and its members in making fast and committed decisions. Although not mandatory, physical co-location is most optimal from a team dynamics perspective. But even when not working co-located, a team needs a shared workspace, including all modern communication facilities required to overcome the physical distance as good as possible.

Within the workspace a team should be able to focus on value-adding activities. All overhead and administrative work is kept to a bare minimum. This includes the storage of information. Teams require fast access to all team information, in order to create, maintain and share it, and speed up all decisions that will be made upon it. That's why teams prefer visual management techniques. A shared workspace has many information radiators [Cockburn, 2002]. Information radiators limit the time to convey information and focus on the team as a unit, which is crucial when performing complex work.

A task overview, team definitions, standards and agreements, process artifacts and progress trends are made accessible and visible within the shared workspace by posting them on the room walls; on white boards, flip charts or other means. This includes all information the team deems appropriate to visualize, such as designs and models, impact analyses, impediments, the definition of Done, the development standards, etc.

Upon entering the room all of the information is readily available, the room radiates it towards the interested reader. The reader is not forced to enter electronic systems, get authorizations, authenticate, search for it, search for the most recent version of it, or even enquire about it. Teams maintain all crucial information in this visualized way to *share* it within and beyond the team members, and use it to inspect and adapt.

The information is not static. It constantly reflects the current state of affairs, where the current state might be used to project forecasts for the future.

A shared visual workspace optimizes transparency and reduces the length of information exchange drastically.

2.6.2 Self-organization

Scrum thrives on the daily collaboration of the three peer roles. Each role has clear accountabilities within the team as well as towards the organization. The Scrum Team and within it the Development Team are self-organizing units of people.

Self-organization is not just the degree of freedom that is allowed. Self-organization is not about delegation. Self-organization *is*, it happens. Self-organization is not about enabling or empowerment, there is no higher authority that grants it. The ability to actually self-organize requires the removal of many existing barriers that prevent people from communicating, interacting, achieving insights and collaborating. This is how external authorities are most effective; by removing organizational or procedural barriers to better facilitate teams.

Self-organization is not about anarchy or limitless freedom. Self-organization has and requires boundaries, boundaries within which self-organization happens. The Scrum rules are one of the primary boundaries within which a team self-organizes its work:

- The Development Team collaboratively selects work as ordered and expressed by the Product Owner, collaboratively creates actionable activities for their Sprint forecast and re-plans the work on a daily basis within a time-boxed Sprint to optimize the outcome.
- The Product Owner interacts with users, stakeholders and product management to identify the most valuable work, and relies on the cross-functional Development Team(s) for the actual delivery of it in Increments of product. Stakeholders help in shaping the future product at every Sprint Review.
- The Scrum Master has no direct interest in scope, budget, delivery or tasks but coaches and facilitates the complete ecosystem in using Scrum to manage these factors.

People organized in teams have the highest cohesion, deepest trust and most effective interconnections when the size of the team numbers around five to seven. Although Scrum sets an expectation of Development Team size to be between three and nine, there's no formal process need to enforce this. Through self-organization a team will adjust its size autonomously until optimal performance is reached. This will even happen across multiple teams working together. There is no external body who knows how to organize work better than the people actually undertaking the work.

In his book 'Drive' [Pink, 2009] Daniel Pink elaborates on the scientific evidence of what motivates people. He describes how 'self-directiveness', the ability for people to direct their own work, is one of three crucial motivators in cognitive, creative work. 'Mastery' and 'Purpose' complete it. Together they make out what Pink identifies as the third drive, the model for human motivation that follows the first drive of surviving and the second drive of industrial-like Taylorist schemes implementing 'carrots and sticks' rewards. The self-organization of Scrum is thus confirmed as crucial for the motivation of the players in creative work requiring cognitive skills.

However, autonomy and self-organization don't resolve all problems. Some problems go beyond the self-organization of the Development Team. Scrum calls those 'impediments'.

The general definition of an impediment is an *'obstruction; hindrance; obstacle'*. An impediment in Scrum is a factor that blocks the team in its creation of a valuable version of product in a Sprint, or that restricts the team in achieving its intrinsic level of progress. It is the accountability of the Scrum Master to remove impediments.

The Scrum concept of 'impediments' however is not a replacement for the traditional escalation procedures. An impediment is only an impediment if it surpasses the self-organizing capabilities of the team, if it cannot be tackled within the self-organizing ecosystem.

Let's illustrate this with the example of a team conflict, a conflict between team members.

A team might have problems in resolving an inner-team conflict and call the conflict an impediment, expecting the Scrum Master to remove it for them. In other words, they expect the Scrum Master to resolve the conflict.

However, working as a team inevitably includes getting to know each other, finding ways of building product versions together, exploring different ways to collaborate, finding consensus over differing ideas, outgrowing the desire for personal heroism. In her book, 'Coaching Agile Teams' [Adkins, 2010], Lyssa Adkins elaborates on 'constructive disagreement' as a necessity for teams. This lowest level of conflict connects with the 'built-in instability' observed and described by Takeuchi and Nonaka [Takeuchi & Nonaka, 1986] as the fertile ground for successful complex product development. It is a natural part of the freedom given to a group of people to jointly discover the best ways to move forward, in the absence of an external authority that prescribes the solution.

Conflicts are a natural part of working with people, of working as a team.
It is an essential part of self-organization. If a team raises an inner-team
conflict with the Scrum Master, one should wonder what the real problem
is. Is it the Scrum Master's role to resolve the conflict? Or would that be
an undesired intervention in the self-organizing ecosystem, undermining
future honesty, learning and self-improvement? How can the Scrum Master
facilitate self-organization? Is it by offering teams an excuse, an external
decision to hide behind?

A Scrum Master, as the promoter of Scrum and self-organization, considers
how to help a team work out their problems themselves and offer any tools,
training and insights on how best to do this, on how to self-develop.

2.6.3   Empirical process control

New product development is a complex activity in itself and it serves to
deliver complex products in complex circumstances.

One perspective on the degree of 'complexity' relates to the number of
parameters, variables and events that influence an activity and its course.
In product development some of the more commonly known parameters
are user expectations and requirements, skills, availability and experience
of people organized in teams, technology, technical integrations, market
conditions and competition, regulations and dependencies.

However, it is not only the number of known parameters that is important,
but also the *available* knowledge as well as the *required* knowledge of these
parameters. What is the level of detail required to comprehend a variable as
well as the future behavior of that variable? Even if a parameter is known,
the level of detail may be too deep to be able to manage and control it.
And then, of course, the behavior of the parameter is still not necessarily
predictable. A known variable may still behave completely differently to
what is expected.

'Complexity' is also dependent on the nature of the activity itself. The exact and detailed outcomes of product development are hard to describe and predict before or even at the beginning of the actual development. The combined steps, tasks and activities that make out the actual work aren't predictable with any degree of high precision. People perform them, and the involvement of people is dependent on many circumstances. And then there's also working with technology itself, where technology evolves constantly and is dependent on the particularity of an organization's environment.

The steps, tasks and activities of product development aren't predictable to a high degree of precision because they are not repeatable. Every 'product' being built that is non-mechanistic or non-industrial is unique. New technologies emerge, new interfaces need to be built, new plug-ins are used, new integrations need to be set up, new insights and techniques for development are discovered regularly, while the work is already taking place.

The degree of dynamism of a problem or activity requires the right process to be in place in order to have the right control over the activity:

■ In an *open loop system*, all of the variables are gathered upfront because they need to be presented to the system as input, before in a single run a number of steps are performed resulting in a predicted outcome. In order to be able to predict outcome and the elapse time, this type of process control assumes a high degree of predictability of the variables that influence the process as well as of the process activities themselves.

Figure 2.10 Open loop system

To gain control over large or complex problems, using the open loop thinking, subsystems are created where each subsystem is a separate open loop system. The input of each subsystem is the output of the previous subsystem. In situations of increased turbulence and frequent change, deviations and variances will accumulate across the chain of subsystems, inherently far beyond acceptable levels, and only to be detected at the end of the final subsystem.

Predictive plans are expressions of the industrial paradigm and implementations of open loop thinking. Predictive plans can only include known variables, and their *expected* behavior. Predictive plans create the illusion that the behavior of the known variables is precisely understood and that other variables are non-existent. Predictive plans invite lengthy upfront consideration of all elements that should be part of the plan, and in a complex context thus attempt to foresee the unforeseeable. In order to control non-predicted variables or unexpected behavior, weighty procedures are required to check, maintain and update the predictive plan.

■ In a *closed loop system*, the actual outcome of the system is regularly compared to the desired outcome, in order to eliminate or gradually diminish any undesired variances. Not all variables and parameters need to be known precisely and in detail upfront, as the process applies self-correction and takes into account new or changing parameters. This technique of regular inspections requires and creates transparency. The real situation is inspected, and exposed, so that the most appropriate adaptations can be undertaken to close the gap between the effective and the expected outcomes. The people performing the inspections, the player-inspectors, need clear and agreed standards in order to carry out their inspections. Hence the need for transparency of the process and all its variables for all players involved.

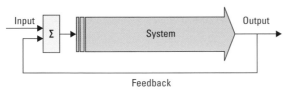

Figure 2.11 Closed loop system

Scrum acknowledges that the complexity of product development requires the right process, i.e. closed loop feedback. Scrum replaces the open loops of traditional processes with the *empiricism* of closed loop systems. Scrum implements regular opportunities for inspection and adaptation, so the players can learn from an inspection, gather feedback over the results and improve. Scrum brings reality-based control to complex work.

Scrum implements two specific closed-loop feedback cycles. A Sprint forms an 'inspect and adapt' cycle that wraps the 24-hours 'inspect and adapt' of the Daily Scrum:

■ At *the Daily Scrum* the Development Team inspects its progress and plans its upcoming work within the container of the Sprint. They use the Sprint Backlog and the Sprint Goal, as initially laid out in Sprint Planning, and a progress trend to consider the remaining work. It assures they don't get out of sync with each other in the team and with the Sprint Goal for more than 24 hours.

■ A *Sprint* is a cycle that starts with forecasting the work and ends with reflections on what was actually built, the product Increment, and how it was built, the process, the team interactions and the technology.

The events of Scrum set the frequency of the inspection and adaptation, where the artifacts contain the information to be inspected and adapted:

Event	Inspection	Adaptation
Sprint Planning	• Product Backlog (Past performance) (Availabilities) (Retrospective Commitments) (Definition of Done)	• Forecast • Sprint Backlog • Sprint Goal
Daily Scrum	• Sprint Progress (toward the Sprint Goal)	• Daily Plan • Sprint Backlog
Sprint Review	• Product Increment • Product Backlog (& progress) • Market & business conditions	• Product Backlog
Sprint Retrospective	• Team & collaboration • Technology & development • Definition of Done	• Actionable improvements (next Sprint)

Figure 2.12 Empiricism in Scrum

Scrum foresees these formal events as opportunities to inspect and adapt to the actual situation, so that the art of empiricism is performed no later than at the time of these events. This should not stop team members from checking for improvements and progress whenever required. In a world of the high dynamism that leads to using the Scrum framework it would be very strange if teams did not capitalize on new information and insights that improve their work life as soon as possible.

None of these events was designed for reporting purposes. All events in Scrum are designed to be forward-looking. The ability to adapt defines the level of agility achieved.

Inspection without adaptation is pointless in Scrum. All Scrum events are intended to be forward-looking, as opportunities to shape the future.

■ 2.7 THE SCRUM VALUES

Scrum, as has been demonstrated, is a framework upon which people and organizations develop a working process that is specific and appropriate to their time and context. The rules and principles of Scrum all serve empiricism, or empirical process control, as the most optimal way to deal with complex challenges in complex circumstances.

There is however more than the rules and the principles. Scrum is more about behavior than it is about process. The framework of Scrum is based upon five core values [Schwaber & Beedle, 2001]. Although these values were not invented as a part of Scrum, and are not exclusive to Scrum, they do give direction to the work, behavior and actions in Scrum.

> Scrum is a framework of rules, principles and... values.

In a Scrum context, our decisions, the steps we take, the way we play the game, the practices we include and the activities we undertake within Scrum, should all re-enforce these values, not diminish or undermine them.

2.7.1 Commitment

The general definition of 'commitment' is "*the state or quality of being dedicated to a cause, activity, etc.*". It can be illustrated by a team's trainer stating, "I could not fault my players for their commitment" (although they might have just lost a game).

This describes exactly how commitment is intended in Scrum. Commitment is about dedication and applies to the actions and the intensity of the effort. It is not about the final result, as this in itself is often uncertain and unpredictable for complex challenges in complex circumstances.

Yet, there was a widely spread misinterpretation of the word commitment in a context of Scrum. This originates mainly from the past expectation of

Figure 2.13 The Scrum Values

the Scrum definition that said teams should 'commit' to a Sprint. Through the lens of the traditional, industrial paradigm this was wrongly translated into an expectation that all scope selected at Sprint Planning would be completed by the end of the Sprint, no matter. 'Commitment' was wrongly converted into a hard-coded contract.

In the complex, creative and highly unpredictable world of new product development, a promise of exact scope against time and budget is not possible. Too many variables influencing the outcome are unknown or may behave in unpredictable ways.

To better reflect the original intent and connect more effectively to empiricism, 'commitment' in the context of scope for a Sprint was replaced with 'forecast'.

However, commitment still is and remains a core value of Scrum:

The players commit to the team. Commit to quality. Commit to collaborate. Commit to learn. Commit to do the best they can, every day again. Commit to the Sprint Goal. Commit to act as professionals. Commit to self-organize. Commit to excellence. Commit to the values and principles stated in the Agile Manifesto. Commit to create working versions of product. Commit to look for improvements. Commit to the definition of Done. Commit to the Scrum framework. Commit to focus on value. Commit to finish work. Commit to inspect and adapt. Commit to transparency. Commit to challenge the status-quo.

2.7.2 Focus

The balanced but distinct accountabilities of Scrum enable all players to focus on their expertise.

The time-boxing of Scrum encourages the players to focus on what's most important now without being bothered by considerations of what might stand a chance of becoming important at some unknown point in the future. They focus on what they know now. YAGNI ('You Ain't Gonna Need It'), a principle from eXtreme Programming, helps in retaining that focus. The players focus on what's imminent as the future is highly uncertain and they want to learn from the present in order to gain experience for future work. They focus on the work needed to get things done. They focus on the simplest thing that might possibly work.

The Sprint Goal gives focus to a period of 4 weeks, or less. Within that period, the Daily Scrum helps people collaboratively focus on the immediate daily work needed to make the best possible progress towards the Sprint Goal.

2.7.3 Openness

The empiricism of Scrum requires transparency, openness, and honesty. The player-inspectors want to check on the real current situation in order to make sensible adaptations. The players are open about their work, progress, learnings and problems. But they are also open for the people aspect of work and working with people; acknowledging people to be people, and not 'resources', robots, cogs or replaceable pieces of machinery.

The players are open to collaborate across disciplines, skills, function and job descriptions. They are open to collaborate with stakeholders and the wider environment. Open in sharing feedback and learning from one another.

They are open for change as the organization and the world in which they operate change; unpredictably, unexpectedly and constantly.

2.7.4   Respect

The broader Scrum ecosystem thrives on respect for people, their experience and their personal background. The players respect diversity. They respect different opinions. They respect each other's skills, expertise and insights.

They respect the wider environment by not behaving as an isolated entity. They respect the fact that customers change their mind. They show respect for the sponsors of their initiatives by not building or keeping functions that are never used and that increase the cost of the product. They show respect by not wasting money on things that are not valuable, not appreciated or might never be implemented or used anyhow. They show respect for users by fixing their problems.

All players respect the Scrum framework. They respect the accountabilities of Scrum.

2.7.5   Courage

The players show courage by not building stuff that nobody wants. Courage in admitting that requirements will never be perfect and that no plan can capture reality and complexity.

They show the courage to consider change as a source of inspiration and innovation. Courage to not deliver undone versions of product. Courage in sharing all possible information that might help the team and the organization. Courage in admitting that nobody is perfect. Courage to change direction. Courage to share risks and benefits. Courage to let go of the feint certainties of the past.

The players show courage in promoting Scrum and empiricism to deal with complexity.

They show courage to support the Scrum Values. The courage to take a decision, act and make progress, not grind. And even more courage to change that decision.

1   'Object-Oriented Programming, Systems, Languages & Applications'
2   31% indicated not to be following any methodology. 21% indicated they were doing iterative development.

3 Tactics for a purpose

Since its first formal description in 1995 the definition of Scrum has gradually evolved via small functional updates. The basic elements are still the same, as are the principles and rules that bind them together. But the mandatory prescriptions of Scrum grow... lighter, as the evolution of the Scrum Guide [Schwaber & Sutherland, 2017] shows.

The evolution is to describe 'what' is expected, i.e. the purpose of the rules, from an understanding of their 'why', as opposed to instructing 'how' to exactly apply the rules.

The previous chapter describes the rules to playing the game of Scrum. Those rules of the Scrum framework leave room for different *tactics* to play the game, tactics that are at any time right-size and can be fitted to context and circumstances. It's as in all games and sports, everyone plays by the same set of rules, yet some are more successful than others. Success depends on many factors, and not all are equally controllable by the players themselves, but success is certainly influenced by the tactics chosen to play the game.

It is like selecting good practices from a collection of such good practices and turning them into best practices by applying and tuning them to a specific context. When referred to as a 'process', Scrum is a *servant* process, not a *commanding* process. Scrum does not say what practices to apply, or not. Scrum helps discover whether they work, but leaves it to the players to keep on doing them or changing them.

There are many tactics to use within Scrum. Good tactics serve the purpose of Scrum. Good tactics re-enforce the Scrum values, rather than undercut them. When applied well, the resulting system is still recognizably… Scrum.

Let's take a closer look at some examples to clarify the difference between tactics and rules:

■ 3.1   VISUALIZING PROGRESS

A good illustration of an evolution of the Scrum framework towards more lightness is the elimination of burn-down charts as mandatory.

Looking at the rules of Scrum, including the need for transparency, which is crucial to the process of inspection and adaptation, and self-organization, it is clear 'why' it is important to visualize progress. Self-correction is difficult to achieve without tracking *and* visualizing progress.

The former obligation, however, to use burn-down charts for that purpose (the 'how') has been removed from the definition of Scrum. The form or format of the visualization is no longer prescribed. It is replaced by the mere, but explicit, expectation that progress on the mandatory Scrum artifacts of Product Backlog and Sprint Backlog is visualized (the 'what').

Find an example of a Sprint Burn-down chart (figure 2.7) in section 2.5.3 ("Tracking progress"). Sprint Burn-down charts are a great self-management instrument for a Development Team within a Sprint.

Following is an example of a Release Burn-down chart, a way to track and visualize progress for a Product Backlog, or part of a Product Backlog, serving a specific goal. The visualization supports the Product Owner in the communication with the stakeholders, the users and the wider product management organization. A Release Burn-down chart and the visual forecast included, enables conversations about balancing time and scope based on actually delivered results.

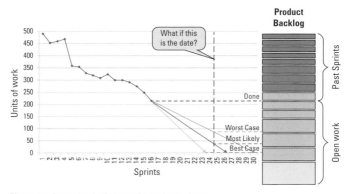

Figure 3.1 Example of a Release Burn-down chart

Burn-down charts are a great way to play the game and are suitable in many situations. Yet, they have been turned into a non-mandatory, good practice.

Yes, it's Scrum if both Product and Sprint Backlog exist and a visualization of their progress is available, accessible and clear. But there are multiple good practices for such visualization. It may be a burn-down chart with open effort. It may be a Cumulative Flow Diagram. It may be as simple as a Scrum Board. For the progress on Product Backlog it may also be a burn-up chart, e.g. in assumed value.

■ 3.2   THE DAILY SCRUM QUESTIONS

Scrum suggests that in the Daily Scrum every player of the team answers three questions with regards to the progress of the team towards its Sprint Goal (*Done? Planned? Impediments?*).

But even if the players answer the questions, they can still limit it to an individual status update. They might use the walls or the Scrum Board for reporting purposes. They might just make sure that they simply answer the three questions. This may be because of people's inability to look beyond the suggestion of Scrum to answer the questions. The perceived rules are formally followed without understanding the 'why'.

Is the team merely seeing Scrum as a methodology? Or is the team using Scrum as a framework for discovery and collaboration? It doesn't help much whether they formally answer the three questions, or not, if they don't actually listen and talk to each other. It doesn't help much if they don't reveal the information to optimize their shared work plan for the next 24 hours against the Sprint Goal. Maybe they use the event only as a formal obligation, a mental remainder of the industrial paradigm. Maybe they feel pressured to make sure all their micro-tasks are logged and cover themselves against possible blame. In doing so, however, they miss the opportunity to gain insight in the real situation, to inspect it and to adapt to it, fluently and rapidly.

Inspection without adaptation is pointless in complex and changing environments. The goal of the Daily Scrum is to share information, and to re-plan the Development Team's collective work so that they progress in the best possible way towards the Sprint Goal. The team sets its own format to do so, within the boundary of keeping it to 15 minutes, or less. That should be the background from which the Daily Scrum is used, regardless whether these are the questions that are addressed, not blindly go through the questions from a 'best practice' viewpoint.

Did you know that a Daily Scrum is not necessarily a Daily Stand-up?

Daily Stand-up is the practice described in eXtreme Programming [Beck, 2000] that serves the same purpose as the Daily Scrum in Scrum. But eXtreme Programming tells participants to do it standing up.

Scrum has no obligation to do it standing up. However, it is a good tactic, especially to keep the time-box within 15 minutes.

■ 3.3 PRODUCT BACKLOG REFINEMENT

Refinement of the Product Backlog is an on-going activity during a Sprint in which the Development Team and the Product Owner look at Product Backlog currently ordered for the next Sprints. There is a growing certainty that the items are actually going to be implemented.

As items come closer in time, teams might want to unveil dependencies, understand better what is expected from the work, decide on a shared approach for its development or help a Product Owner understand the development impact at a functional level. Collaborative refinement of Product Backlog, and the additional knowledge that emerges from the refinement conversation, increases the chances that the work might actually, or more easily, be pulled into a Sprint when it is presented at a future Sprint Planning.

Product Backlog refinement is not an official, time-boxed event. The ambition of Scrum is to remain simple, yet sufficient. The ambition of Scrum is to help people and teams discover specific practices that may or may not be appropriate in their specific context. Product Backlog refinement is an activity that many teams undertake to smoothen their Sprints, and reduce turbulence in the first days of a Sprint. A typical feature of Product Backlog refinement activities is that estimates of effort or cost get set, or are revised. Other teams may need less precision at Sprint Planning or have a relationship with the Product Owner that's less about accuracy. They cope without it, or do it less formally, do it without explicitly naming or consciously planning this activity. They would perceive it as optional or even as an overhead if it was a mandatory event having a defined time-box and time of occurrence.

Product Backlog refinement is a great activity within a Sprint, a good tactic to collaboratively manage Product Backlog. Some can do without however.

■ 3.4   USER STORIES

In eXtreme Programming [Beck, 2000] requirements were captured in 'User Stories'. User Stories were written on index cards and describe functional expectations from a user's perspective. Bill Wake, an early practitioner of eXtreme Programming, suggested the 'INVEST'[1] acronym as a simple way to remember and assess whether or not a User Story is well formed: Independent, Negotiable, Valuable, Estimable, Sized appropriately, Testable.

User Stories typically describe a feature as a 'Story' from the perspective of the 'User'. The advantage of taking the user's perspective to describe the system or application requirement is the focus on the value of the work for that user.

Index cards are easy to move around on, or remove from, a planning board, as an information radiator. Another advantage of using physical index cards for stories is the limited space for textual descriptions and details. It ensures that it is incomplete by design and in this way makes sure that conversation takes place. As a User Story comes closer in time, and the chances grow that it will get implemented, it necessarily requires conversation to discover additional details. More information may be added to the card, and some of this may be expressed as acceptance criteria for the User Story, the confirmation that the Story is well implemented. Such acceptance criteria are typically written on the back of the card.

A Product Backlog in Scrum serves to provide transparency to *all* work that a team needs to do. This comprises more than just functional requirements. Although the User Story format may be used for other types of requirements than functional, there is no natural fit. It tends to shift the focus to the syntax instead of the information to be conveyed.

There is no obligation in Scrum to use the User Story-format for Product Backlog items. It even creates the risk of neglecting other important work that needs to be undertaken, or it might force teams to spend more time and energy on using the 'right' format, thus creating waste. However, for functional items on the Product Backlog, User Stories can be very good, a great tactic.

■ 3.5 PLANNING POKER

Planning Poker is an estimation technique invented by James Grenning during an eXtreme Programming project where he felt too much time was spent on merely producing estimates.

In Planning Poker, a team has a discussion about a requirement, after which every team member decides on an estimate for the requirement by picking a value from a set of poker cards. Poker cards typically use an exponential scale like the Fibonacci sequence (1, 2, 3, 5, 8, 13, 21, 34, 55, ...). All team members keep their chosen value to themselves until everybody has chosen a value. They then reveal their estimates at the same time, after which they engage in a conversation over possible differences. This cycle is repeated until agreement is reached, a joint understanding of the requirement. Estimates are relative to each other and are expressed in an abstract unit like (Story) points, or even gummy bears as in early eXtreme Programming projects.

In Scrum, estimates on Product Backlog items are the responsibility of the Development Team. As part of transparency and collaboration, it is required to have honest and unbiased estimates from the complete Development Team, a collective perspective including all skills and expertise present within the team.

Although not mandatory, Planning Poker is a good tactic for that principle. But don't forget that the ultimate intention is to invoke an honest discussion about the estimates, because this results in a good understanding of the work attached to implementing the discussed item.

■ 3.6   SPRINT LENGTH

Scrum only sets the maximum length of a Sprint, i.e. no more than four weeks. This maximum length ensures that nobody is deprived of the right to adapt the future plans for the product at least every 4 weeks. Additionally, the team does not stay locked away in a container for too long, at the risk of losing grip on the changing world.

Sprint length holds a balance between retaining focus to get a substantial amount of work done and opportunistic adaptiveness, weighed against other factors, like technological uncertainties and learning opportunities.

In an empirical process like Scrum, control objectives are presented to the system and, via closed-loop feedback, results are regularly inspected against these objectives to adapt work materials, tasks and processes. Skilled inspectors, the roles foreseen by Scrum, carry out inspections at an appropriate frequency, so the focus and time required to create valuable output are balanced against the risk of allowing too much variance in the created output.

In addition to transparency, frequency is an important factor in empiricism. The Scrum events determine the frequency of the inspections and adaptations in Scrum, with the Sprint being a container event, the outer feedback loop that wraps the feedback loop of the Daily Scrum, and the feedback loops of the development practices applied within the Sprint.

There is a clear tendency to move to shorter Sprints. Although not a formal obligation, one-week Sprints feel like an acceptable minimum.

Let's have a look at this by presuming that a team does one-day Sprints.

All Scrum events, as opportunities to inspect and adapt, take place in the same duration of one day, and are thus organized at a very high frequency. When actually trying to perform all events, the team spends an unreasonable amount of time inspecting and adapting the tiniest of work packages. The frequency gets in the way of producing value.

The danger is even higher that a team will focus merely on its daily work and progress, losing sight of the bigger picture. They will take no time to inspect and adapt the overall process, or probe for ways to improve quality or connect to an overarching goal and objectives. They will just try to get more product out the door, every day.

Sprint length also determines the frequency at which the Product Owner and the Development Team consult with stakeholders over a working version of the product. The purpose is to share all information needed to help the Product Owner make decisions about the future of the product. In the case of one-day Sprints, stakeholder buy-in will be more difficult to achieve, let alone allow capturing and adapting to enterprise, market and strategic changes.

Sprint length should take into account the risk of losing a business opportunity because Sprints are too long. If your business is so volatile that you risk losing opportunities by spending more than one day in the container of a Sprint, please do one day Sprints. But be careful of burning the inspection mechanisms at such high frequency.

Prevent Scrum from turning into a new name for the old rat race, where no workplace humanization takes place. Organize work such that it is sustainable, indefinitely.

> Consider your Sprint length as a tactic to play Scrum. See how it works and adapt accordingly, bearing in mind stability, heartbeat and sustainable pace. And if you want to release sooner than by the end of a Sprint, nothing in Scrum says you can't. The purpose of time-boxed Sprints and the Sprint Review event remain intact regardless.

■ 3.7   HOW SCRUM SCALES

The mandatory elements of Scrum have been described, as well as the rules to play the game of Scrum, the rules that cohesively tie those elements together. The rules remain consistent and are independent of the scale at which Scrum is organized.

Scrum promotes simplicity. Scrum promotes clear accountability and peer collaboration to deal with unpredictability and formulate answers to complex problems.

Simplicity, bottom-up accountability and collaboration were not at the core of many enterprises when scaling their organizations and their work upon the industrial paradigm. The main challenge in scaling Scrum lies not in fitting Scrum into the existing structures, but to revise the existing structures via a bottom-up understanding, implementation and growth of Scrum, while keeping the base rules of the game intact and respecting them. Adapt the organization to Scrum, not the other way around.

There are some tactics that allow Scrum to be played on a larger scale, depending on the context.

3.7.1 Single-team Scrum

The simplest situation for delivering product with Scrum is to have a Product Backlog capturing the desirements for the product and have one team deliver Increments of product in time-boxed Sprints.

The Development Team has all the skills to turn several Product Backlog items into a releasable product Increment per Sprint, guided therein by the definition of Done. The Development Team manages its work autonomously via Sprint Backlog and safeguards direction and alignment via the Daily Scrum. The Product Owner provides right-time functional and business clarifications. The Scrum Master coaches, facilitates and serves the team and the organization.

The single team is a Scrum Team, having one Product Owner, one Development Team and one Scrum Master. In order to deliver product functions that provide start-to-finish user value, the Development Team is what is typically called a 'feature team'.

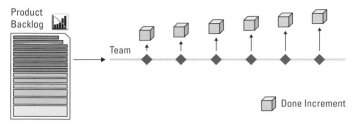

Figure 3.2 Single-team Scrum

The biggest challenge lies in having all development skills collaborating as one team. But if that problem is overcome, the Sprint Review is fully transparent, an important prerequisite to make the empirical approach of Scrum work. The team uses the Sprint Retrospective to improve itself.

3.7.2 Multi-team Scrum

For larger products or faster results, the need to create and release a product with multiple teams may surface.

The multiple teams deliver one product. They work on the same Product Backlog. The collective system has one Product Owner, multiple Development Teams and one or more Scrum Masters. Each Development Team designs its Sprint Backlog for their work from the forecast. Each Development Team self-adapts via a Daily Scrum and assures integration of the work with the other Development Teams.

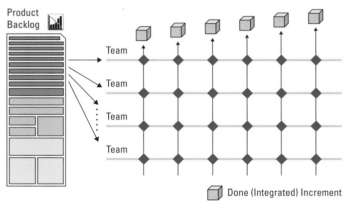

Figure 3.3 Multi-team Scrum

The need for full transparency at the Sprint Review remains, complete transparency over the version of product as released or to be potentially released. The product Increments cannot have undone, hidden work left. However, the multiple teams are jointly building the same product. Only a fully *integrated* Increment assures the Product Owner, and the stakeholders, of complete transparency.

The multiple teams self-organize, within the boundaries of the Scrum rules and principles. When working in a construct of multi-team Scrum, i.e. several teams creating and sustaining the same product, the teams self-organize against the expectation of creating an integrated Increment no later than by the end of a Sprint.

Regular communication across the multiple teams is required, throughout the Sprint, to align the teams' work plans against the objective of creating an integrated Increment. The teams extend the principle and purpose of the Daily Scrum to a cross-team level and organize *Scrum-of-Scrums* events.

In order to keep the whole optimized, the Scrum-of-Scrums happens before the individual Daily Scrums. The most appropriate representatives of the Development Teams gather to exchange development information, primarily focusing on the state of integration of the product. Subsequently, each Development Team can optimally re-plan and adjust its individual Sprint Backlog within the bigger multi-team ecosystem. As a result, the multiple teams optimize their joint progress towards an integrated Increment of product, no later than by the end of each Sprint. The technically sound Increment can be released upon the assessment by the Product Owner considering whether it has the right level of usefulness, not hindered by open, unknown development work still to be performed.

The multiple teams work against the same quality criteria for the product as expressed in the definition of Done. The multiple teams might find it easier to work on the same Sprint length to simplify planning, integration, releasing and reviewing of the work. Additional work will be foreseen in their individual Sprint Backlogs to keep their work integrated and healthy.

In order to work on different Sprint lengths, a clear agreement and policies are crucial to assure all work is kept integrated continuously, a green tree policy that takes precedence at all times. If anything breaks the whole, that needs to be fixed first, indefinitely. As a result, each individual team or each combination of teams can (potentially independently) derive a releasable Increment from the shared codebase. *Shared Sprint Reviews still make a lot of sense though.*

All accountabilities defined by Scrum are fulfilled. The whole of the system is recognizably Scrum. To deliver product Increments that provide start-to-finish user value the whole is a 'feature system'. Regardless the composition of the individual teams, they collectively deliver integrated Increments of product, no later than by the end of a Sprint.

3.7.3   Multi-product Scrum

Depending on the functional or technical inter-dependency of multiple products, there may be a need for the planning and implementation of the products to be aligned and synchronized.

Each product has a Product Owner. For each product a Product Backlog exists with one or multiple teams to create, deliver and sustain it. Each product eco-system is a single-team Scrum or multi-team Scrum instance.

From the accountabilities of Scrum, it is clear that alignment and synchronization primarily happens at the level of the Product Backlogs through the respective Product Owners. Individual Product Backlogs are additionally ordered upon optimization of the product line, the product suite, program or portfolio considerations. The Product Owners, thereby assisted and facilitated by the organization, incrementally manage their Product Backlogs on the basis of shared information and shared progress.

Technical and development dependencies are handled inner-Sprint by the Development Teams of the different product hubs in a networked, non-hierarchical spirit.

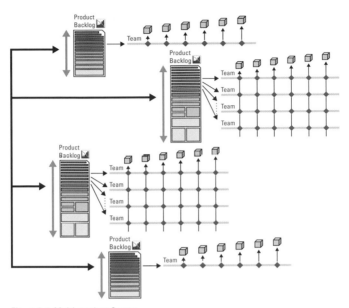

Figure 3.4 Multi-product Scrum

Many more scaling problems, and therefore scenarios, exist. There is not one silver bullet solution. Scrum promotes bottom-up thinking with top-down support to discover and emerge what works best for you, your organization and your context.

1   See http://xp123.com/articles/invest-in-good-stories-and-smart-tasks/ for details.

4 The future state of Scrum

■ 4.1 YES, WE DO SCRUM. AND...

Scrum emerged in the 1990's from the work and discovery of Ken Schwaber and Jeff Sutherland. They critically analyzed and reflected on practices that at that time were considered as common in software development, their own professional experience, successful product development strategies [Takeuchi & Nonaka, 1986] and process control theory. The sum of their findings became Scrum [Schwaber, 1995] and was formally presented to the public in 1995 [Sutherland, 1995]. In the years that have passed since the publication of the 'Manifesto for Agile Software Development' [Beck, et.al., 2001] in 2001, Scrum became the most applied Agile framework worldwide.

Yet, Scrum has remained a light and simple way to organize complex work and address complex challenges based upon the Agile principles and ideas. The unique combination of the clear definition and the low-prescriptive nature of Scrum are paramount to its success, now and in the foreseeable future. Scrum, as an organizational framework, can wrap various product development practices or might render existing practices superfluous. Scrum is likely to reveal the need for new practices. The benefits of Scrum will be greater when complemented by improved or revised development, product management, people and organizational practices. When done well, the sum will still be Scrum.

Over the first two decades of its existence, organizations have primarily used Scrum for the IT and technology aspects of software development. For many IT people worldwide, the Scrum framework has become a proven solution. Despite the great results, like Agile overtaking waterfall and the gorilla position of Scrum, there is room for improvement. There is a need to take it further.

Challenging the status quo of the industrial paradigm has improved continuous learning in dealing with many *technological* uncertainties in the IT domain and has helped many organizations to shift from organizing work in projects and regain a focus on products. In many organizations the understanding has been restored that software and product development is a creative and complex activity. But the focus is often still on 'how' the products are built. It is time to elaborate on the achieved results and take your Scrum to the next level.

There is a myriad of possibilities to play Scrum, a myriad of practices that can be wrapped by Scrum, and the results and performance of the work managed with Scrum are influenced by many factors. The co-location of people influences it. The energy, dedication and joy of the people-players influence it. The level of self-organization influences it. The fact whether people have to multi-task influences it. The availability of development and testing automation, tools, platforms and practices influences it.

A crucial aspect is the cross-functional thinking that goes beyond the walls of the IT and software department, through the enterprise. Remember that Agile is driven by business opportunities. From having implemented Scrum for the 'how' of product delivery, adding more focus now to 'what' needs to be built is crucial. That shift will help organizations discover the power of the possible product, over the restrictions of the predicted product, reduce the amount of product being built, instead of merely optimizing the way that the product is being developed. *See section 4.2.*

There is a myriad of techniques and practices to play Scrum and that Scrum can wrap. But more than process and techniques, moving from the old, industrial paradigm to the new Agile paradigm is about an organizational upgrade. The common enthusiasm with teams that arises from doing Scrum is unlikely to be sufficient for a deep organizational transformation. For a lasting effect the common bottom-up enthusiasm needs to be supported and facilitated by upstream adoption. *See section 4.3.*

■ 4.2 THE POWER OF THE POSSIBLE PRODUCT

The value that products bring can be greatly increased if we deal better with *what* is being delivered; the requirements, features and functions.

In turbulent enterprise, business and market circumstances the certainty and stability of requirements is low. Improved and active collaboration with business owners and product managers is a natural next step in optimizing product delivery. Only the people accountable for the business value of the products can help overcome the unavoidable absence of full agreement over features and requirements. And more than ever these product people need the flexibility to capitalize on unforeseen opportunities in order to build the best possible product at the right time. What is appreciated today might not be what people are looking for tomorrow.

The Scrum framework allows people to give up on trying to predict the unpredictable, as the framework supports dealing with answers, solutions and competing ideas that emerge while building and evolving a product, while the product is already being used. Scrum renders the question of whether issues were thought of upfront as irrelevant. Requirements as the input for the product delivery eco-system are no longer expected to be complete, final and exhaustive. Scrum helps by accepting - and embracing – the fact that the final agreement on the 'what' of the product only gets resolved *while* creating it. Scrum helps by validating internal decisions frequently against the usage of the product in the marketplace. Scrum opens the door for, and promotes, frequent functional releases as a better way to progress, since they have regular feedback from customers built in and do not merely accumulate assumptions via sequential open loop systems. When connection to the marketplace is tight, real user feedback can be easily incorporated as emerging requirements in the living artifact that Product Backlog is.

In Scrum, the Product Owner is the only one deciding what to build (next). The Product Owner consolidates the work from the Development Team(s) into a next release or version of the product for the marketplace. The mandate of the Product Owner influences the level of improvement and agility an organization achieves with Scrum. On top of the mandate, a Scrum Product Owner needs a close connection to all related product management domains: marketing, communication, sales, legal, research, finance, support, etc. The Product Owner ultimately acts as a Product-CEO.

It is in that sense equally essential to promote multi-disciplined collaboration across organizational walls within product management. The capability to adapt these parts of an organization leverages the use of Scrum for *enterprise* agility. In a globalizing world of ever-increasing internal and external unpredictability, adopting a mindset of empiricism and adaptiveness is beneficial to entire organizations.

Employing Scrum is not about renaming or slightly reworking old techniques that are rooted in the industrial paradigm. Scrum does not require product people to fill Product Backlog like they did with traditional requirements documents. Nor does it suffice for analysts to act as proxies for the product people if they lack a mandate, stakeholder backing, budget responsibility and real user representation.

Scrum Sprints are the core of overall business agility in generating a regular flow of improvements, learnings and various other sources of value; value to the stakeholders, value to the users and consumers of the products, value to the people creating and maintaining them.

Ultimately, an enterprise and its markets become a self-balancing continuum, with players contributing across barriers, domains, skills and functions. Organizations can discover, experiment and deliver opportunities from an end-to-end perspective in the fastest possible way with Scrum.

■ 4.3 THE UPSTREAM ADOPTION OF SCRUM

When adopting Scrum, the broader organization is impacted. Period.

Issues that go beyond the Scrum Teams will come up and need to be taken care of in order to gain the full benefit of Scrum, to better facilitate the Scrum Teams and thereby improve the complete space of product delivery. Organizational opportunities and improvement areas are discovered through the application of Scrum.

Organizations wanting to use Scrum to progress on their journey of agility should be aware that this will not be achieved by implementing Scrum just for the sake of it. Scrum has the potential of being a *tool* to be Agile at an organizational or enterprise level. Scrum is not designed to be just a new IT process, but rather as a framework of rules, principles and values to enable organizations to capitalize on the unforeseeable. Scrum enables fast adaptation to follow the market and provide competitive advantage (again).

A vast majority of organizations unfortunately act as if they still reside in the land of *Mediocristan*. The characteristics for that 'state' of society, as described by Nassim Nicholas Taleb in his book 'The Black Swan' [Taleb, 2007], are that success has a direct relationship to the hours or effort spent on non-scalable, repetitive work. Taleb describes how Mediocristan has become an illusion of the past, and has been replaced by *Extremistan*, where success depends on the 'production' of ideas and the elaboration of unpredicted singularities. Scrum has what it takes to beam up the inhabitants of Mediocristan to Extremistan so they become at least 'a' player in Extremistan, and potentially a leader, a giant. Scrum can be the engine for adapting so fast that it's up to your competitors to respond to the change you cause. Leading the game comes within reach, outplaying the rest of the field, being the giant.

But it starts with accepting, or rather embracing, that we operate in a market state of Extremistan. It starts with accepting, or rather provoking, that our organizations must change not to fade. The industrial fundaments on which a majority of them are constructed have been invalidated. *Our iceberg is melting*, is the metaphor in the tale of Holger Rathgeber and change expert John P. Kotter [Kotter & Rathgeber, 2006]. Ignoring or belittling the huge shift towards complexity is an important cause of a lack of upstream adoption for Scrum and it limits the benefits realized by playing the game of Scrum. It undermines your future leadership, and even survival.

In larger organizations, Scrum Teams and their Scrum Masters have limited or no control over the bureaucratic obligations related to the delivery and the release of products. Often teams have to operate on the basis of compliancy expectations and ceremonial rules that were put in place as part of the industrial paradigm. They are being maintained beyond the actual experience of building products and lack of success. In many cases they have grown out of step with the rapid evolutions that are so typical for today's markets, external circumstances and internal organizational evolutions.

Nevertheless, the experience with Scrum in a vast majority of these cases is excellent and lives up to a sense of common sense. The inhabitants of the house of Scrum appreciate Scrum because it thrives on and creates much enthusiasm. No surprise that this is exactly why *downstream adoption* is generally huge.

One would expect that proven results, improved figures and increased delivery of value would lead to more upstream interest and supported adoption of the real thing. Experience contradicts this expectation.

Your organization deserves active and explicit upstream support and promotion of Scrum. Think about operational IT management, sales divisions, delivery managers, product management departments and hierarchical CxO management.

It takes a sense of urgency, and the acceptance that there indeed *is* urgency. It starts by accepting the inconvenient truth that no comfort, certainty and control comes from traditional predictions and plans. Comfort comes from reality, from proven experience, observable working results and empirical data instead of static and gamed information. The traditional formalisms of the industrial paradigm have not resulted in improved execution. Requirements change, unexpected requirements appear, priorities shift.

Upstream adoption is a matter of management. Management is not useless just because Scrum has no explicit role for them. Scrum neither has prescriptions, artifacts, events or roles for lots of other interesting and useful tasks or activities within organizations.

The goal of a lasting Scrum transformation on the journey of Agility is to get managers involved in the game through a structured, iterative-incremental approach to organizational change. The goal for managers is to re-invent themselves, their role and their work. Such an approach thrives upon urgency for improvement, meanwhile capitalizing on the bottom-up enthusiasm that exists over Scrum. Such a change doesn't address organizational areas in a mass-production or cascaded waterfall-way. A typical waterfall transition starts with an enterprise introducing Scrum and resolving the 'problem' of cross-functional teams first. This often reveals a lack of engineering facilities and support, so that domain is tackled next. After addressing the engineering area, an enterprise might want to increase business involvement. And so on. Depending on the size of the enterprise, it can easily take one to three years per area. In the end, it is a series of linearly sequenced open-loop systems, offering no chances of success in high complexity.

An organizational transformation based on Scrum addresses enterprise domains concurrently, producing Increments of change. A transformation changes how an organization works, rather than adds work on top of what people already do. An Agile transformation of adopting Scrum simplifies how work is done, maximizes the work not done. A transformation follows no straight direction; it is bottom-up, top-down, left-right, right-left, inside-out, outside-in. At the same time. An Agile transformation is based on the premise that people are naturally Agile, have the natural ability to adapt. The process of Scrum follows people. Structure should follow process.

Cross-functional change teams implement small steps in the domains in parallel while the overall effects of the incremental steps are measured. The regular inspections of enterprise or product-level measurements form the base for informed decisions on the next steps and practices in the various domains. The vertical silo-like departments become dimmed. Barriers get removed. Communities emerge. Authority moves down the line. Accountability grows. Organizational structures and processes re-emerge. Agility occurs.

And remember, agility can't be planned, dictated or copied, as agility is unique and has no end-state.

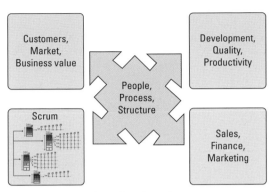

Figure 4.1 Enterprise Scrum Transformation

The future state of Scrum will no longer be called 'Scrum'. What we now call Scrum will have become the norm, and organizations have re-emerged around it.

Annex A: Scrum Glossary

Burn-down Chart: a chart showing the decrease of remaining work against time.

Burn-up Chart: a chart showing the increase of a parameter, e.g. value, against time.

Daily Scrum: a daily event, time-boxed to 15 minutes or less, to re-plan the development work during a Sprint. The event serves for the Development Team to share the daily progress, plan the work for the next 24 hours and update Sprint Backlog accordingly.

Definition of Done: the set of expectations on quality that a product Increment must exhibit to make it releasable, i.e. fit for a release to the product's users.

Development standards: the set of standards and practices that a Development Team identifies as needed to create releasable Increments of product no later than by the end of a Sprint.

Development Team: the group of people accountable for all evolutionary development work needed to create a releasable Increment no later than by the end of a Sprint.

Emergence: the process of the coming into existence or prominence of unforeseen facts or knowledge of a fact, a previously unknown fact, or knowledge of a fact becoming visible unexpectedly.

Empiricism: the process control type in which decisions are based on observed results, experience and experimentation. Empiricism implements regular inspections and adaptations requiring and creating transparency. *Also referred to as 'empirical process control'.*

Forecast: the anticipation of a future trend based on observations of the past, like the selection of Product Backlog deemed deliverable in the current Sprint or in future Sprints for future Product Backlog.

Impediment: any hindrance or obstacle that is blocking or slowing down the Development Team and cannot be solved through the self-organization of the Development Team itself. Raised no later than at the Daily Scrum, the Scrum Master is accountable for its removal.

Increment: a candidate of releasable work that adds to and changes previously created Increments, and – as a whole – forms a product.

Product: any tangible or non-tangible good or service consisting of a cohesive combination of features and functions that provide end-to-end value (start-to-finish) in solving a specific problem for the people employing the product (users). *Defines the span of: Product Owner, Product Backlog and Increment.*

Product Backlog: an ordered, evolving list of all work deemed necessary by the Product Owner to create, deliver, maintain and sustain a product.

Product Backlog refinement: the recurring activity in a Sprint through which the Product Owner and the Development Team add granularity to future Product Backlog.

Product Owner: the person accountable for optimizing the value a product delivers, primarily by managing and expressing all product expectations and ideas in a Product Backlog. The single representative of all stakeholders.

Scrum (n): a simple framework for complex product delivery (1); a simple framework for addressing complex challenges (2).

Scrum Master: the person accountable for fostering an environment of Scrum by guiding, coaching, teaching and facilitating one or more Scrum Teams and their environment in understanding and employing Scrum.

Scrum Team: the combined accountabilities of Product Owner, Development Team and Scrum Master.

Scrum Values: a set of 5 fundamental values and qualities underpinning the Scrum framework; commitment, focus, openness, respect and courage.

Sprint: an event that serves as a container for the other Scrum events, time-boxed to 4 weeks or less. The event serves getting a sufficient amount of work done, while ensuring timely inspection, reflection and adaptation at a product and strategic level. *The other Scrum events are Sprint Planning, Daily Scrum, Sprint Review and Sprint Retrospective.*

Sprint Backlog: an evolving plan of all work deemed necessary by the Development Team to realize a Sprint's goal.

Sprint Goal: a concise statement expressing the overarching purpose of a Sprint.

Sprint Length: time-box of a Sprint, which is 4 weeks or less.

Sprint Planning: an event marking the start of a Sprint, time-boxed to 8 hours or less. The event serves for the Scrum Team to inspect the Product

Backlog considered most valuable at that time and design that forecast into an initial Sprint backlog against the Sprint Goal.

Sprint Retrospective: an event marking the closing of a Sprint, time-boxed to 3 hours or less. The event serves for the Scrum Team to inspect the Sprint that is ending and establish the way of working for the next Sprint.

Sprint Review: an event marking the closing of the development of a Sprint, time-boxed to 4 hours or less. The event serves for the Scrum Team and the stakeholders to inspect the Increment, the overall progress and strategic changes in order to allow the Product Owner to update the Product Backlog.

Stakeholder: a person external to the Scrum Team with a specific interest in or knowledge of a product that is required for the further evolution of the product.

Time-box: a container in time of a maximum duration, potentially a fixed duration. *In Scrum all events have a maximum duration only, except for the Sprint itself which has a fixed duration.*

Velocity: popular indication of the average amount of Product Backlog turned into an Increment of releasable product during a Sprint by a specific (composition of a) team. Velocity serves primarily as an aid for the Development Team of the Scrum Team to forecast Sprints.

Annex B: References

Adkins, L. (2010). *Coaching Agile Teams, A Companion for ScrumMasters, Agile Coaches, and Project Managers in Transition.* Addison-Wesley.

Beck, K. (2000). *Extreme Programming Explained – Embrace Change.* Addison-Wesley.

Beck, K., Beedle, M., v. Bennekum, A., Cockburn, A., Cunningham, W., Fowler, M., Grenning, J., Highsmith, J., Hunt, A., Jeffries, R., Kern, J., Marick, B., Martin, R. C., Mellor, S., Schwaber, K., Sutherland, J., Thomas, D. (February 2001). *Manifesto for Agile Software Development.* http://agilemanifesto.org/

Benefield, G. (2008). *Rolling Out Agile at a Large Enterprise.* HICSS'41 (Hawaii International Conference on Software Systems).

Cockburn, A. (2002). *Agile Software Development.* Addison-Wesley.

Giudice, D. L. (November 2011). *Global Agile Software Application Development Online Survey.* Forrester Research.

Hammond, J., West, D. (October 2009). *Agile Application Lifecycle Management.* Forrester Research.

Kotter, J., Rathgeber, H. (2006). *Our Iceberg Is Melting, Changing and Succeeding Under Any Conditions.* MacMillan.

Larman, C. (2004). *Agile & Iterative Development, A Manager's Guide.* Addison-Wesley.

Larman, C., Vodde, B. (2009). *Lean Primer.* http://www.leanprimer.com

Moore, G. (1999). *Crossing the Chasm, Marketing and Selling Technology Products to Mainstream Customers (second edition).* Wiley.

Pink, D. (2009). *Drive: The Surprising Truth About What Motivates Us.* Riverhead books.

Schwaber, K. (October 1995). *SCRUM Software Development Process.*

Schwaber, K., Beedle, M. (2001). *Agile Software Development with Scrum.* Prentice Hall.

Schwaber, K., Sutherland, J. (November 2017). *The Scrum Guide.* http://www.scrumguides.org.

Standish Group (2002). Keynote on Feature Usage in a Typical System at XP2002 Congress by Jim Johnson, Chairman of the Standish Group. Results from a study of 2000 projects at 1000 companies.

Standish Group (2011). *Chaos Manifesto (The Laws of Chaos and the Chaos 100 Best PM Practices).* The Standish Group International.

Standish Group (2013). *Chaos Manifesto 2013: Think big, act small.* Standish Group.

Sutherland, J. (-) Oopsla '95 - Business Object Design and Implementation Workshop. http://www.jeffsutherland.org/oopsla/schwaber.html

Sutherland, J. (October 2011). *Takeuchi and Nonaka: The Roots of Scrum.* http://scrum.jeffsutherland.com/2011/10/takeuchi-and-nonaka-roots-of-scrum.html

Taleb, N. N. (2007). *The Black Swan - The Impact of the Highly Improbable.* Random House.

Takeuchi, H., Nonaka, I. (January-February 1986). *The New New Product Development Game.* Harvard Business Review.

Verheyen, G. (December 2011). *The Blending Philosophies of Lean and Agile.* Scrum.org (https://www.scrum.org/resources/blending-philosophies-lean-and-agile).

Verheyen, G., Arooni, A. (December 2012). *ING, Capturing Agility via Scrum at a large Dutch bank.* Scrum.org (https://www.scrum.org/resources/ing-capturing-agility-scrum-large-dutch-bank).

VersionOne (2011). *State of Agile Survey. 6th Annual.* VersionOne Inc.

VersionOne (2013). *7th Annual State of Agile Development Survey.* VersionOne Inc.

Wiefels, P. (2002). *The Chasm Companion. A Fieldbook to Crossing the Chasm and Inside the Tornado.* Wiley.

About the author

 **Gunther Verheyen** (gunther.verheyen@mac.com) is a
longtime Scrum practitioner (2003). After a standing
career as a consultant, he became partner to Ken
Schwaber and Director of the Professional Scrum
series at Scrum.org (2013-2016). Gunther engages with
people and organizations as an independent Scrum
Caretaker.

Gunther ventured into IT and software development after graduating in
1992. His Agile journey started with eXtreme Programming and Scrum
in 2003. Years of dedication followed, years of employing Scrum in
diverse circumstances. As from 2010 Gunther became the inspiring force
behind some large-scale enterprise transformations. In 2011 he became a
Professional Scrum Trainer.

Gunther left consulting in 2013 to found Ullizee-Inc and partner exclusively
with Ken Schwaber, Scrum co-creator. He represented Ken and his
organization Scrum.org in Europe, shepherded the 'Professional Scrum'
series and guided Scrum.org's global network of Professional Scrum
Trainers. Gunther is co-creator to Agility Path, EBMgt™ (Evidence-Based
Managing of Software) and the Nexus framework for Scaled Professional
Scrum.

Since 2016 Gunther continues his journey as an independent Scrum Caretaker; a connector, writer, speaker, humanizer. His services build on 15 years of experience, ideas, beliefs and observations of Scrum, expressed in re-vers-ify, an act of people re-imagining their Scrum to re-emerge their organization.

In 2013 Gunther published the first edition of *'Scrum – A Pocket Guide'*, by Ken Schwaber recommended as 'the best description of Scrum currently available' and 'extraordinarily competent'. In 2016 the Dutch translation was published as "Scrum Wegwijzer". In 2017 the German translation was released as "Scrum Taschenbuch". This second edition is the base for additional translations.

When not traveling for Scrum and humanizing the workplace, Gunther lives and works in Antwerp (Belgium).

Find Gunther on LinkedIn at https://www.linkedin.com/in/ullizee, on Twitter as https://twitter.com/ullizee or read more of his musings on Scrum on his blog, https://guntherverheyen.com/.